Pinch of Nom

AIR FRYER LIGHT & EASY

Pinch of Nom
AIR FRYER
LIGHT & EASY

ALL-NEW, TIME-SAVING MEALS UNDER 500 CALORIES

BLUEBIRD

CONTENTS

INTRODUCTION
6

BREAKFAST
33

FAKEAWAYS
55

BAKES and ROASTS
103

LIGHT BITES
143

SWEET TREATS
177

EASY TO HALVE INDEX
200

NUTRITIONAL INFO
210

INDEX
214

ACKNOWLEDGEMENTS
222

HELLO

Welcome to our brand-new collection of delicious air fryer recipes – all under 400 and 500 calories!

Thanks for joining us on our latest air-fryer adventure! We absolutely love our air fryer and use it every chance we get, so we thought it only right that we share all our most up-to-date recipes, tips and tricks with you! The first edition was a huge hit, and we've had so much fun creating a whole new bounty of recipes – this time with an even lighter twist. We've made every recipe simple so you can jump straight in, even if you didn't pick up the first book or you're new to air frying. All you need is your air fryer, some tasty ingredients and a little curiosity. We know life is busy, so each and every recipe is easy to cook AND full of flavour, so you can still enjoy all the meals you love (and a few new ones!) without any of the fuss. To top it all off, we know you asked about servings and we listened: this time, we've made sure all the meals can be easily halved to serve two.

WHY AIR FRYER?

We couldn't resist another air-fryer cookbook, because honestly, we just can't get enough! This gadget has totally changed the way we cook, and we're always discovering new ways to make mealtimes quicker and tastier. It saves us so much time, whether we're serving up a satisfying soup for lunch, crisping up sides for speedy weeknight dinners, or rustling up a tasty breakfast ahead of time to encourage us to get out of bed that bit faster in the morning! If you ask us, an air fryer is a must-have in every kitchen.

Just like the first edition, we've filled this cookbook with recipes that are simple to follow whether you're an air-frying pro or a complete beginner. You can flick through to find your favourites and get cooking in no time.

From simple **Cheesy Beans and Soldiers** on page 36 right through to creamy **Chicken and Coconut Curry** on page 63, we've got every craving covered… and then some!

The beauty of using an air fryer is that it gives dishes that irresistible crunch we all love, with only a little spray or no oil at all, so you can really get creative with your low-calorie cooking. To make sure you're able to cook every recipe in this book to perfection, we've also popped in plenty of hints and tips, as well as an easy-to-follow air fryer to oven conversion chart on page 28.

For each chapter, we've focused on crowd pleasers that never get boring. You can always rely on cosy **Creamy Sausage Gnocchi** (page 108), mix things up with fragrant **Katsu Cod** (page 60), or rustle up something a little different for lunch with our **Pizza Crumpets** (turn to page 154 for those). We've also added plenty of sweet treats that you might not have tried in your air fryer before, like our fluffy **Cinnamon Doughnut Holes** on page 188.

We hope *Air Fryer: Light & Easy* inspires you to try new flavours and shows you just how fun air-frying can be. We promise you, there's so much here to get excited about! And, of course, none of this would be possible without our amazing community, so once again we'd like to say a huge thank you to you all! Your appreciation means the world to us, and we can't wait to see what you make first. And second! And third! Without further ado… ready, set, fry!

Kay x Kate

ABOUT AIR FRYERS

Like everyone else, we've been blown away by how popular air fryers have become over the last few years. At first, we weren't sure whether they'd be just another fad gadget that quickly went out of fashion, but they've turned out to be a handy bit of kit that lots of us can't live without!

When we decided to do this book, we promised we'd make sure every recipe worked in every different air fryer. Before you start cooking up an air-fried feast, here are a few things you'll need to know...

HOW DO AIR FRYERS WORK?

Air fryers work by circulating a powerful blast of hot air around the basket or drawer. This cooks food really quickly, locking in flavour and making everything mouthwateringly crispy! They'll give you a really satisfying, deep-fried crunch, without the need for lots of high-calorie oil or cooking fat – which is what makes them perfect for slimming-friendly cooking.

Often, cooking something in your air fryer can save you from having to turn on your oven at all. Since air fryers are much smaller than traditional ovens, they're also more energy efficient to use. Although they can be a bit of an investment, if you regularly use your air fryer, it might well save a few pennies on your energy bills in the long run.

It doesn't matter if you have a traditional air fryer or a halogen air fryer; both versions will work for the recipes in this book. There are also a few models out there that come with a paddle to stir food while it cooks – in general, this can just be removed, but check your product manual if you're not sure.

WHAT AIR FRYER DID WE USE?

To develop the recipes for this book, we used a Dual Zone Air Fryer with a 9.5-litre capacity and 2470W of power.

Don't panic if the air fryer we've used sounds totally different to the one you've got waiting on your kitchen counter! Keep an eye out for hints and tips throughout the book to help you adapt the recipes to suit whatever you're working with.

DOES THE WATTAGE OF YOUR AIR FRYER MATTER?

It's well worth making a note of how the wattage of your air fryer compares to the one that we used, as this does have a slight impact on how quickly food cooks. You can find this out by looking for the wattage on the product label, in the booklet that came with your air fryer, or on the manufacturer's website.

Typically, most air fryers will fall between 1200W and 3000W of power. Smaller air fryers will usually have lower wattages, whereas large capacity models tend to need a bit more power. The wattage of your air fryer makes the biggest difference when you first pop your food in the basket. When you add cold food into a preheated air fryer (or oven), the internal temperature will drop a few degrees. Since a more powerful appliance heats up more quickly, it'll climb back up to the desired temperature in less time than a lower-wattage model. This is why food will cook a little bit faster in a higher-wattage air fryer.

All this talk of basket size and wattages can get a bit confusing, but don't worry! Once you've checked how your air fryer compares to the one we've used, you'll be able to use the cooking times on our recipes as a guideline.

If your air fryer is more powerful, you may need to cook the dishes for a little less time, and if it's less powerful, cook for a little longer. The good thing about air fryers is that it's okay to open the drawer/lid to check on your food as it cooks. This means you can keep a close eye on your meal, and tweak the cooking time as required to get perfect results.

COOKING FUNCTIONS, TEMPERATURES *and* PREHEAT SETTINGS

For the recipes in this book, we'll tell you what temperature to set your air fryer to, and how long to cook it for. If your air fryer offers a choice of cooking functions, select the general 'air-fry' setting.

Some air fryers don't allow you to manually adjust the cooking temperature; in this case, check your product manual to find out the temperature settings of each pre-programmed cooking function. From there, you'll be able to select the best match for the recipe you're making.

Lots of air fryers come with a preheat function, and will beep to tell you it's time to add in the food. We know that some models don't have a preheat function however, so if yours doesn't, just set it to the required temperature and let it heat up for a few minutes before popping the food inside.

DIFFERENT BASKETS, DRAWERS *and* SHELVES

From baskets to dual drawers and from grill shelves to paddles, we've seen it all while we were putting this book together! There's always a way to make a recipe work with the air fryer you've got.

Some of the dishes in this book are air-fried straight into the drawer, while others may tell you to use a small ovenproof dish or ramekin. We found that air-fryer accessories, such as silicone or disposable liners, came in handy time and time again when we needed to adapt a recipe. You'll find more details of any bits and bobs that we recommend in Our Favourite Kit on pages 22–6.

AIR-FRYER CLEANING *and* CARE

It can't be avoided… your air fryer has to be cleaned between each use! To keep you safe, any buildup of grease or food crumbs needs to be fully removed before you start cooking. Check whether any parts can be placed in the dishwasher, otherwise you should find that removable drawers and baskets are easy to wash by hand. Silicone or disposable liners are handy if you want to make cleaning even easier.

We've dropped a handy step-by-step video on how to clean your air fryer, along with lots of other resources on our website. Scan the QR code below to visit the site for air-fryer accessories recommendations, buying guides and more.

THE FOOD

As a classically trained chef, Kate has always loved recreating dishes and putting an original spin on classic recipes. This is how the very first Pinch of Nom recipes came to be, and it's this passion that means we can continue to bring fresh new flavours to you today. Kate and her small team of trusted recipe developers love nothing more than getting into the kitchen and experimenting with ingredients until some Pinch of Nom magic is created!

It's always been our mission as a recipe team to make it easy to cook healthy, homemade food, and this book is no exception. It's been another exciting learning curve for us to work with just one kitchen gadget again, and there's been lots of trial, error and taste-testing along the way! We've taken things one ingredient at a time to find the best ways to adapt familiar favourites, and create totally new recipes. We hope that you'll be able to tell just how much fun we've had experimenting with cooking trademark Nom flavours, in a newer, speedier, crispier way!

To save on time and pennies, we've kept everything as stripped back as possible, and we've relied on fuss-free ingredients that you can use across multiple dishes. From time to time, you might find a less common ingredient that adds something really special to a dish, but we'll always try to make sure you get to use it again somewhere else.

If you've followed Pinch of Nom since day one, you'll know that it's hugely important to us that absolutely anyone can pick up our books and give cooking a go. All of the recipes we've picked suit any level of cooking skill, so even if you've never used an air fryer before, you'll have no trouble with our slimming-friendly breakfasts, lunches, dinners, sides and desserts.

Although we haven't added our usual categories in the book– because all of them are lower calorie – the recipes all qualify for our Everyday Light or Weekly Indulgence categories. This means that the under-400-calorie mains and under-200-calorie light bites and sweet treats (including accompaniments) are Everyday Light. The 400–500-calorie mains and 200–300-calorie light bites and sweet treats (including accompaniments) qualify as Weekly Indulgence.

We've made this cookbook just as quick and convenient as air-frying itself, by clearly flagging all of our vegetarian and vegan dishes, and adding notes where ingredient swaps can be made. You'll also spot that we've dropped hints and tips throughout.

RECIPE ICONS

OUR RECIPE ICONS

HIGH PROTEIN

These recipes are packed with extra protein, with at least 20% of the calories in each serving coming from a source of protein. The benefit of this is that they keep you fuller for longer, give you an extra burst of energy, and help you hit your fitness goals!

EASY TO HALVE

Our community loves cooking for two, so we've made it super-easy to adapt any savoury recipe to make two portions. All the relevant recipes have an 'Easy to Halve' icon. The Easy to Halve index on pages 200–208 does all the hard work so you don't have to – it includes ready-halved quantities and any additional tips needed to make it super-easy to serve two or four people.

KCAL *and* CARB VALUES

All of our recipes have been worked out as complete meals, using standardized portion sizes for any accompaniments, as advised by the British Nutrition Foundation. Carb values are included for those who need to measure their intake.

GLUTEN-FREE RECIPES

We have marked gluten-free recipes with a 'Gluten Free' icon. All these recipes are either free of gluten or we have suggested gluten-free ingredient swaps of common ingredients, such as stock cubes and Worcestershire sauce. Please check labelling to ensure the product you buy is gluten-free.

FREEZABLE RECIPES

Look out for the 'Freeze Me' icon to indicate freezer-friendly dishes. The icon applies to the main dish only, not the suggested accompaniments.

STANDARD FREEZING *and* REHEATING GUIDELINES

For most recipes, you'll be able to follow our standard freezing and reheating guidelines below (we'll let you know if a recipe requires more specific instructions):

- Allow food to cool and then freeze as soon as it is cold enough.
- Place in a container or bag that is suitable for freezing.
- Add a label telling you the name of the recipe and the date you're freezing it.

The general consensus is that you can keep food frozen for around 6 months, although after 3 it'll start to lose its flavour.

You should reheat and eat defrosted food within 24 hours. Please don't reheat frozen food until it has defrosted thoroughly in a fridge or microwave. NHS guidelines (correct at the time of writing) state that you should reheat food until it reaches 75°C/167°F and holds that temperature for 2 minutes. Always make sure it's piping hot throughout (you should stir while reheating to ensure this).

Keep cooked rice in the fridge no longer than 1 day before reheating it, or you can freeze it and defrost thoroughly in the fridge before reheating. Always make sure you reheat rice until it is piping hot, and never reheat it more than once.

If you're ever unsure about freezing and reheating a recipe safely, we'd strongly advise referring to the official NHS guidelines.

All of the calculations and dietary indicators are for guidance only and are not to be taken as complete fact without checking ingredients and product labelling yourself.

KEY INGREDIENTS

PROTEIN

Lean meats are a great source of protein, providing essential nutrients and keeping you feeling full between meals. In all cases where meat is used in this book, we'd recommend using the leanest possible cuts and trimming off all visible fat. In many of our recipes you'll find that you can switch the type of protein for whatever meat you prefer. This especially applies to any mince recipes; turkey, beef or pork mince are easily interchangeable – just be mindful that you may need to adjust air-frying times to suit! Fish is also a great source of protein, and it's naturally low in fat. Fish provides nutrients that the body struggles to produce naturally, making it perfect for lots of our super-slimming recipes. And don't forget, vegetarian protein options can always be used instead of meat in all of the recipes in this book.

HERBS *and* SPICES

We love a bit of spice! One of the best ways to keep your food interesting when changing ingredients for lower-fat/sugar/calorie versions is to season it well with herbs and spices. Mixed spice blends, either shop-bought or homemade, are great for adding flavour in a pinch. Don't be shy with spices – not all of them burn your mouth off! We've added a spice-level icon to the recipes in this book, so you know what to expect. The beauty of cooking dishes yourself is you can always adjust the heat to your liking – add more or less chilli to suit. Always taste your food before adding extra spicing; spices, vinegars, mustard and hot sauces should be added gradually, to taste.

STOCKS, SAUCE *and* THICKENERS

When you remove fat from a dish, flavours can dwindle. Adding spices is one way to boost flavours, but often the level of acidity in a recipe is much more important. When it comes to balancing and boosting flavours in our dishes, we love to use vinegar, soy sauce, fish sauce, Worcestershire sauce or Henderson's relish. One of Pinch of Nom's essential ingredients is the humble stock cube or stock pot; they add instant flavour and they're so versatile. We use various flavoured stock cubes and pots throughout this book, but there's always an option if you can't get your hands on the exact ones we've used. It's worth noting that sauces, stock cubes and pots are often high in salt, so you may want to swap for reduced-salt versions.

Reduced-sugar ketchup isn't just great for topping chips, it also adds a rich depth of flavour to soups, stews or pasta sauces. We've also popped in a few recipes for our own low-calorie sauces and dips, like our Indian-Style Sweet Potato Fries and Raita on page 144.

From breakfasts to fakeaways and midweek dinners, we often use either syrup or honey to give dishes a touch of sweetness, without drying them out (you'll be wanting to turn to page 95 for our Bacon and Maple Meatballs!)

We're often asked for tips on how to thicken soups, sauces and gravies. In the pre-slimming days, we wouldn't have thought twice about using a few tablespoons of flour to thicken liquids. Nowadays, we're always on the lookout for lower-calorie and gluten-free options. Letting liquids reduce is a good way of thickening sauces without adding anything extra. As the moisture evaporates, the flavours get more concentrated, too, so the end result will taste even better.

REDUCED-FAT DAIRY

Substituting high-fat dairy products with clever alternatives can make a dish instantly lower in calories. You'll find that we'll often use reduced-fat cream cheese or spreadable cheese rather than the higher-fat versions.

TINS

Don't be afraid to bulk-buy tinned essentials! Beans, tomatoes and sweetcorn all come in handy time and time again. Using tinned ingredients can really help to keep costs down, and you'll never know the difference.

FROZEN FRUIT and VEG

Frozen fruit and veg make great filler ingredients and are perfect low-cost alternatives when fresh ingredients aren't always necessary. Most of the time they're already peeled and chopped, too, so they save time as well as money. You can just throw them in alongside your other ingredients.

PULSES, RICE and BEANS

High in both protein and fibre, keeping a few tins of beans and pulses in the cupboard is never going to do any harm! Rice is a fantastic filler and a great accompaniment to so many Pinch of Nom recipes.

BREAD, WRAPS *and* PASTRY

A great source of fibre, wholemeal bread is filling and versatile. Wholemeal rolls, panko breadcrumbs, sourdough, wraps... we've used them all this time around! We often go for gluten-free breads as they tend to contain fewer calories and less sugar, so they're an easy swap when you want to shave off a few calories.

POTATOES

It wouldn't be right to talk about air-frying without mentioning the humble potato. No matter what variety you prefer, one thing's for sure: your air fryer will crisp it to perfection. Some of our favourites from this time around include Smoky Halloumi and Sweet Potato Bake on page 114 and Crispy Chilli Potato Salad on page 164, and there are plenty more that prove you can never have too many spuds on standby! Chopped, sliced, mashed or filled, the 'beep' will tell you when this versatile root veg is fluffy in the middle and ready to serve as a light lunch or side dish.

EGGS

Eggs are protein-rich, tasty and versatile! A simple egg can be used in so many different ways. From baking and binding ingredients together, to having a starring role in our Eggy Bread Toastie on page 41, you'll never go wrong if you have a box of eggs in the house.

LOW-CALORIE COOKING SPRAY

One of the best ways to cut down on cooking with oils and fats is to use a low-calorie cooking spray. A spritz of this will make little difference to the end result of your food, but it can make a huge difference to the calories consumed. Make sure to spray your food directly and toss it to coat evenly, rather than spritzing into the air fryer basket, so you don't damage the non-stick coating inside your appliance.

SWEETENER

There are so many sweeteners out there, it can be tricky to know which is the best substitute for regular sugar. Sweeteners vary in sweetness and swapping them weight-for-weight with regular sugar can give you different results. In our recipes we use granulated sweetener, not powdered sweetener, as it has larger 'crystals'. This can be used weight-for-weight anywhere that you're replacing sugar.

DRIED PASTA and NOODLES

We wouldn't want to live without pasta or noodles! They're not too pricey to stock up on, and they'll keep nicely in the store cupboard until you're ready to transform them into fakeaway favourites and midweek classics, like our Roasted Vegetable Pasta Bake on page 134.

MICROWAVEABLE RICE

Microwaveable rice is a real time-saver, making it a useful staple to have in your kitchen cupboards! It's a filling and fuss-free base for many of the meals in this book, including Spanish-Style Chicken and Butter Bean Rice on page 87, where it soaks up all the delicious flavours of the chicken and spices. We've also used it in our Biryani-Style Turkey on page 71. Popping it in the microwave means perfectly cooked grains every time without the stress of standing over a pan.

SELF-RAISING FLOUR, BAKING POWDER and ROLLED OATS

Whether you're an expert or beginner baker, you'll want to make sure you've got self-raising flour. It's an essential ingredient to guarantee the fluffiness of cakes, muffins and other baked goodies. Sift flour together with baking powder to air-fry scrumptious flavour combinations like our Biscoff and Banana Cakes on page 186. Rolled oats are cracking to have in the cupboard for batch-cookable breakfasts. They're rich in filling fibre that'll fuel you up for the day ahead, or they're just as handy for whipping up sweet snacks and desserts.

NUTS

Nuts are an amazing ingredient to have in your kitchen, adding crunch and flavour (and even a boost of protein!) to both sweet and savoury dishes. We've used them in a range of recipes in this book, including flaky Cashew Macaroons on page 182 and warming Caramelized Baked Apples on page 190. Peanut butter (a cupboard staple!) makes our Peanut Butter Cookies on page 196 delightfully indulgent without being over the top. Nuts also work a treat in breakfast recipes like our Maple, Date and Tahini Granola on page 38.

TINNED FRUIT

Tinned fruit makes whipping up sweet treats quick and simple! It's already prepped and ready to go, saving you time on peeling, chopping and prepping fresh fruit. Even better, it's a smart way of adding natural sweetness and juicy flavour to your desserts while saving on calories. It's a lifesaver for recipes like our Apricot Tarte Tatin on page 178. The fruit caramelizes beautifully in your air fryer to give you a deliciously sticky golden topping, time after time!

DRIED FRUIT

Just like tinned fruit, dried fruit brings natural sweetness and a chewy texture to sweet and savoury dishes alike. We've used it in recipes like Biryani-Style Turkey on page 71, where it adds a subtle sweetness to the spiced turkey, Maple, Date and Tahini Granola on page 38, for a crunchy breakfast treat, and in Spiced Cauliflower and Cranberry Couscous on page 172, for even more flavour and texture.

OUR FAVOURITE KIT

AIR FRYER

It might seem silly to say it, but you'll need an air fryer to make the recipes in this book (although you can convert the cooking times to work in an oven using the chart on page 28). If you're buying your first air fryer, or in the market for a new one, there are so many different models to choose from. Our advice is to pick an air fryer that best suits how many people you're cooking for, and how often you think you'll use it. Choose a larger capacity if you're cooking for a big family, or look for a model with dual drawers if you want to cook your main and sides at the same time. The main thing to remember is that there's always a way to make the recipes in these pages work, even if your air fryer is a completely different size and shape to someone else's.

AIR-FRYER ACCESSORIES

Most air fryers come with all the essential bits of equipment you need to get started. In this section, we've noted down the 'nice to haves' we like to use with our air fryer, but you don't have to buy them all. For even more recommendations and useful resources, scan the QR code on page 11 to visit our online air-fryer guide.

TONGS *and* GLOVES
Unlike an oven, it's okay to open your air fryer drawer or lid to check on your food during cooking. You'll want to protect yourself by wearing heat-resistant gloves to give your air fryer basket a good shake, or by using tongs to safely toss, flip and stir ingredients.

BAKEWARE
Air fryers normally come with bakeware bits like racks, trays and baskets. The best ones for you to buy will depend on the size and shape of your air fryer, so be sure to take note of your air fryer's measurements before shopping around. With a baking tray, baking tin or shallow dish, you'll be able to air-fry lots of our recipes. As always, you want to look out for the ones with a non-stick coating – they'll be nice and easy to clean! For rustling up bakery-inspired goodies that are even in size, it's well worth picking up a silicone muffin mould, or you can buy individual-sized muffin cases if you have a smaller air fryer. For making fluffy loaves like our Pumpkin Bread on page 198, you'll want to pick up a 450g (1lb) loaf tin (we'll always specify if the size of equipment is essential to the success of a recipe, and you'll spot the details listed as 'Special Equipment').

GRILL RACKS *and* SKEWER RACKS
Grill racks and skewer racks are really nifty cooking tools if you want to take your air fryer to the next level, especially if you'll be cooking meat. Racks are designed to elevate ingredients like mouthwatering steaks, crispy-coated chicken burgers or marinated fish, so that they're exposed to hot air from all angles. This is especially good news if you're looking to achieve a gloriously golden crispy coating! Ingredients that are sliced into chunks can be threaded onto skewer racks; you should be able to turn your kebab-style creations during cooking, to make sure everything's nice and evenly grilled.

BASTING BRUSH
A basting brush will always come in handy for preparing meats, fish or anything where you don't want the flavours to dry out. Carefully brush your ingredients to make sure they're fully coated, and the flavouring from your sauce, seasoning or spice mix is evenly distributed. We'll specify where we've used ours throughout the book.

SILICONE LINERS/PAPER LINERS
Liners are an affordable bit of kit that'll help you keep your air fryer in tip top condition, by catching any excess grease while you're cooking. You can buy parchment liners to throw away after each use, but we prefer to wash and reuse silicone liners. They have a much higher temperature resistance than paper versions and they make the clean-up of oily residue even easier! If you have a basket-style air fryer, you can also use a small metal tin instead of a silicone liner. This works well for recipes that might be a bit trickier to lift out for smaller portions.

RAMEKINS
From crème brûlées and soufflés to miniature quiches, there are lots of ways you can get creative with ramekins. They're ideal for keeping ingredients tidy that might otherwise cause a bit of a mess inside of your air fryer, like eggs. Crack a couple into a small dish and they'll bake until they're just right for you, with a soft or hard centre.

MEAT THERMOMETER
Some models of air fryer come with a built-in meat thermometer, which will automatically stop cooking when your food has reached the desired temperature. If your air fryer doesn't have this, you can always use your own meat thermometer to help you double-check the temperature of your food. Always insert at a slight angle through a chunky part of the meat for the most accurate measure!

KITCHEN BASICS

NON-STICK PANS
Even for a cookbook that's mostly air fryer recipes, you'll find yourself reaching for a saucepan now and again, to make sides, sauces and other bits on the hob. The better the non-stick quality of your pans, the fewer cooking oils and fats you'll need to use in order to stop food sticking and burning. Keep your pans in good health by cleaning them properly and gently with soapy water. We recommend picking up a good set of saucepans, a small and a large frying pan.

KITCHEN KNIVES *and* KNIFE SHARPENER
Every kitchen needs a good set of knives. If you can, splurge on some good-quality, super-sharp knives – blunt knives have a habit of bouncing off ingredients, which can make them more dangerous than sharper ones. You'll need to mind your fingers with super-sharp knives too, but you'll be glad you invested when you've got knives that glide through veg, saving you so much time and effort. Keep them nice and sharp so you can carry on slicing and dicing like a pro.

CHOPPING BOARDS

As well as protecting your surfaces, a good set of chopping boards are the key to a safe and hygienic kitchen. We'd suggest picking up a full set of colour-coordinated chopping boards, with separate boards for veg, meat, fish and dairy. They'll make it so much easier to keep your ingredients separate, and most sets are easy to clean and tidy away once the meal prep is sorted.

HOB

We cook on an induction hob from time to time when we're sautéing sauces or other bits of prep that aren't air-fryer friendly. If you have a ceramic/hot-plate hob you may have to cook dishes for a little longer.

FOOD PROCESSOR, BLENDER, STICK BLENDER *and* ELECTRIC WHISK

These are essential pieces of kit for a lot of Pinch of Nom recipes. We like to make sauces from scratch, so a decent blender or food processor is a lifesaver. A stick blender can be used on most occasions if you're looking for something cheaper or more compact. It's well worth the investment for the flavour of all those homemade sauces. An electric whisk is nice to have when you need to whip up a scrummy sweet treat in a hurry.

MIXING BOWLS

A couple of mixing bowls will come in handy time and time again. We'd suggest getting at least two, a smaller one and a large one will see you through most kinds of recipes. Smaller bowls give you more control when you're whisking ingredients and larger bowls mean more room to mix it up.

MEASURING SPOONS

Want to make sure you never get muddled between a teaspoon (tsp) and tablespoon (tbsp)? Pinch of Nom has absolutely, definitely never made this mistake. Honest. But these days we're never without a trusty set of measuring spoons, which help make sure it's not a tablespoon of chilli when it should have been a teaspoon. Just make sure you use a butter knife to level off the spoon – you'll be surprised how much extra you add when the spoonful is heaped.

HEATPROOF JUG

A measuring jug is essential for measuring out wet ingredients. We recommend getting a heatproof version that you can stick in the microwave when needed.

FINE GRATER

Using a fine grater is one of those surprising revelations. You won't believe the difference between grating cheese with a fine grater versus a standard grater. For example, 45g of cheese can easily cover an oven dish when using a fine grater. You can also use it for citrus zest, garlic and ginger – it helps a little go a long, long way.

GARLIC CRUSHER

You'll never miss the faff of finely chopping garlic once you've invested in a garlic crusher. Relatively cheap to pick up, you won't go back after you've squeezed that first clove into a perfect paste. It'll save you so much time and it helps your garlic spread evenly throughout the dish.

WOODEN OR METAL SKEWERS

Threading meat, fish or vegetables onto skewers means they'll leave the air fryer with so much more deliciously juicy flavour. You can keep turning them for even cooking, and you can make sure every inch of your meat is covered with marinade. Be sure to soak wooden skewers in water, so that they don't catch and burn.

TUPPERWARE *and* PLASTIC TUBS

Many of the Pinch of Nom recipes in this book are freezable and ideal to enjoy all over again as tasty, slimming-friendly leftovers. It's a good idea to invest in some freezer-proof tubs – and they don't have to be plastic. For a more eco-friendly solution, choose glass storage containers; just remember to check they're freezer-safe.

*Note on plastic: We have made a conscious effort to reduce the amount of non-reusable plastic, such as cling film, when making our recipes. There are great alternatives to cling film now available, such as silicone stretch lids, beeswax food covers, fabric food covers and biodegradable food and freezer bags.

CONVERSION CHARTS

You'll notice there are no alternative cooking methods included in this book, but that's not to say you can't make most of these recipes in an oven if you prefer. In general, cooking in an oven will give results that are just as delicious, although it will take a bit longer and may be a little less crispy.

To help you convert the recipes to cook in an oven, here's a handy conversion guide:

OVEN	AIR FRYER
10 MINS	8 MINS
15 MINS	12 MINS
20 MINS	16 MINS
25 MINS	20 MINS
30 MINS	24 MINS
35 MINS	28 MINS
40 MINS	32 MINS
45 MINS	36 MINS
50 MINS	40 MINS
55 MINS	44 MINS
1 HOUR	48 MINS

OVEN	OVEN (FAN)	AIR FRYER
190°C	170°C	150°C
200°C	180°C	160°C
210°C	190°C	170°C
220°C	200°C	180°C
230°C	210°C	190°C
240°C	220°C	200°C

INTRODUCTION

AIR-FRYER FAVOURITES COOKING GUIDE

Your air fryer is perfect for cooking all your favourite fresh ingredients in a healthy, delicious way! For those times when you need to rustle up a side of veggies, or fancy a back-to-basics dinner, we've put together a handy chart to help you get started.

Remember, these timings should be used as a guideline only! All air fryers are a little bit different, so take this chart as a starting point, and keep a close eye on your food as it cooks. Feel free to open the drawer or peek inside the basket to make sure you're on the way to crispy, air-fried perfection!

VEGETABLES	TEMPERATURE	TIME
ASPARAGUS	200°C	6–8 MINS
AUBERGINE, SLICED	200°C	12–14 MINS
BEETROOT, QUARTERED	200°C	16–18 MINS
BROCCOLI	180°C	8–10 MINS
BRUSSELS SPROUTS	180°C	8–10 MINS
BUTTERNUT SQUASH, CUBED	200°C	18–20 MINS
CARROTS, SLICED	200°C	12–14 MINS
CAULIFLOWER	180°C	8–10 MINS
CORN ON THE COB	200°C	10–12 MINS
COURGETTE, SLICED	200°C	10–12 MINS
GREEN BEANS	200°C	8–10 MINS
MUSHROOMS	200°C	8–10 MINS
ONIONS, SLICED	180°C	10–12 MINS
PARSNIP, SLICED	200°C	16–18 MINS
PEPPERS, SLICED	200°C	8–10 MINS
SPRING ONIONS	200°C	6–8 MINS
TOMATOES, HALVED	180°C	6–8 MINS

POTATOES	TEMPERATURE	TIME
CHIPS AND WEDGES	200°C	20–25 MINS
JACKET POTATO	200°C	45–50 MINS
ROAST POTATOES	200°C	25–28 MINS
SWEET POTATO, WHOLE	200°C	35–40 MINS

MEAT and POULTRY	TEMPERATURE	TIME
BACON MEDALLIONS	200°C	5–7 MINS
SAUSAGES	180°C	12–15 MINS
CHICKEN BREASTS	180°C	18–20 MINS
CHICKEN THIGHS	180°C	20–22 MINS
WHOLE CHICKEN, MEDIUM	200°C	1 HOUR

FISH	TEMPERATURE	TIME
SALMON	180°C	10–12 MINS
PRAWNS	180°C	6–8 MINS
FISH CAKES	200°C	12–15 MINS
WHITE FISH	200°C	10–12 MINS

*These cooking times were tried and tested in our Dual Zone Air Fryer with a 9.5-litre capacity and 2470W of power.

BREAKFAST

USE GF BREAD

CHERRY COTTAGE CHEESE TOAST

🕒 **5 MINS**   🍳 **10 MINS**   ✕ **SERVES 2**

PER SERVING:
219 KCAL /34G CARBS

- 2 slices wholemeal sourdough, approx. 40g per slice
- 4 tsp honey
- 150g reduced-fat cottage cheese
- 60g cherries, sliced in half and stones removed
- 3–5 fresh mint leaves, finely sliced

All you need to create this scrummy protein-packed breakfast is five ingredients, your air fryer and a spare 15 minutes. We've combined everyone's go-to healthy cheese with juicy, tart cherries and sweet honey on crisp sourdough toast to create a breakfast that almost feels like a dessert. It can easily be made gluten-free with coeliac-friendly bread – and if you're not a fan of cherries, you can switch things up with peaches, blueberries or blackberries.

Spread each slice of bread with one teaspoon of honey.

Pile the cottage cheese onto the bread and place the cherries on top.

Air-fry at 180°C for 8–10 minutes until the toast is crisp, the cottage cheese is turning lightly golden brown around the edges and the cherries are soft.

Sprinkle over the mint and drizzle over the remaining honey.

CHEESY BEANS *and* SOLDIERS

🕐 **10 MINS**   🍲 **20 MINS**   ✕ **SERVES 2**

PER SERVING:
334 KCAL /43G CARBS

low-calorie cooking spray
2 slices wholemeal bread, 37g per slice
40g reduced-fat Cheddar, finely grated
½ medium red onion, peeled and finely diced
1 x 400g tin cannellini beans, approx. 240g drained and rinsed
200g passata
2 tbsp tomato puree
1 tsp granulated sweetener
1 tsp mixed herbs
1 tsp garlic granules
salt and freshly ground black pepper, to taste

This recipe is a hug on a plate, and you've probably got most of the ingredients in your cupboard already... just what you need to start the day. We've coated cannellini beans in comforting tomato sauce – with red onion, mixed herbs and garlic to spice things up slightly. Obviously, the main event is the cheese – reduced fat to save on calories, and generously sprinkled on top for a golden, gooey finish. A posh plate of nostalgia!

Remove the basket from your air fryer and spray the drawer with low-calorie cooking spray. Alternatively, use a silicone liner or tin that fits inside your air fryer basket. Add the two slices of bread and spray again. Cook at 180°C for 4 minutes, then flip and cook for a further 2 minutes.

Sprinkle over 10g of the cheese and continue to cook for 2 minutes. The bread should be golden and crisp and the cheese melted. Remove and leave to one side.

Spray the drawer again, add the onion and cook for 3 minutes.

Add the beans, passata, tomato puree, sweetener, herbs and garlic, then season to taste and stir well. Cook for 7 minutes, then add the remaining cheese and cook for a further 2 minutes until the cheese is melted.

Slice the toast into soldiers and serve with the beans.

USE GF OATS

MAPLE, DATE *and* TAHINI GRANOLA

⏱ **5 MINS**   🍲 **15 MINS**   ✕ **SERVES 10**

PER SERVING:
198 KCAL /23G CARBS

75g tahini paste
50g maple syrup
1 tsp finely grated orange zest
200g porridge oats (not quick cook)
30g pumpkin seeds
30g cashews
1 tsp ground cinnamon
1 tbsp granulated sweetener (optional)
75g chopped dates

TO ACCOMPANY:
100ml skimmed milk (or plant-based alternative) (+ 35 kcal per serving)

Granola... in your air fryer? Yep, you'd better believe it! This delicious and nutritious breakfast is simple and easy to make – ready in just 20 minutes! It's easily adapted to suit your preferences too. We've used tahini paste, dates and cinnamon for a Middle Eastern-inspired twist – but if you'd rather go old school, you can switch out the tahini for any nut butter, and swap the dates for any dried fruit of your choice. We've given you some suggestions in our tips, so breakfast will never be boring again!

Place the tahini paste, maple syrup and orange zest in a bowl and pop in the microwave for a few seconds to melt. Alternatively, melt in a pan on the hob, over a low heat.

Add the oats, pumpkin seeds, cashews, cinnamon and granulated sweetener (if using) to a mixing bowl. Stir in the melted tahini and maple syrup until combined.

Line the air fryer basket with non-stick baking paper, or use a parchment liner or silicone liner. Press the granola mix into the prepared basket.

Air-fry at 160°C for 12–15 minutes, stirring and breaking the mixture into clumps every 5 minutes. The granola is cooked when it is crisp and golden.

Tip the granola onto a tray and stir in the dates while it is still warm. Allow to cool, then transfer to an airtight jar.

Serve with cold milk, or alternatively sprinkle on top of some mixed berries and fat-free Greek yoghurt.

TIPS:
Swap the tahini for peanut butter, the cashews for peanuts and the dates for dried banana chips.

You could also serve with 150g fat-free Greek yoghurt (67 kcal per serving) and 100g mixed berries (30 kcal per serving).

BREAKFAST

EGGY BREAD TOASTIE

⏱ **5 MINS**   🍲 **8 MINS**   ✕ **SERVES 1**

PER SERVING:
397 KCAL /34G CARBS

1 medium egg
1 tsp Dijon mustard
2 slices thick bread, approx. 43g per slice
30g reduced-fat Cheddar, finely grated
25g honey-roast ham, cut into chunks
low-calorie cooking spray
salt and freshly ground black pepper, to taste

Everyone loves a slice of eggy bread, so we've gone one better with this eggy bread toastie. Cooked in under 10 minutes in your air fryer, this innovative toasted sandwich includes two slices of fluffy bread, stuffed with ham and cheese for a salty, oozy filling. Eat it on its own for breakfast or make it into a lunch with a side of salad or chips. Don't forget the coleslaw!

Add the egg to a shallow bowl or plate, season to taste with salt and pepper and beat with a fork.

Spread the mustard onto both slices of bread. Sprinkle 20g of the cheese on one of the slices, mustard-side up, then top with the ham. Place the other slice of bread, mustard-side down, on top.

Place the sandwich into the egg mixture. Leave to stand until half of the mixture has been absorbed by the bread, then flip and let the egg mixture soak into the other side.

Line the air fryer basket with non-stick baking paper and spray with a little low-calorie cooking spray.

Add the sandwich and sprinkle over half of the remaining cheese. Cook at 200°C for 4 minutes. Flip, sprinkle over the rest of the cheese and cook for a further 4 minutes. The toastie should be golden brown and turning crispy. Slice and serve.

PESTO EGG BAGELS

 10 MINS　　 **12 MINS**　　✗ **SERVES 2**

PER SERVING:
307 KCAL / 27G CARBS

1 bagel, sliced in half
1 tbsp green pesto
15g reduced-fat cream cheese
3–5 fresh basil leaves, finely chopped
juice of ½ lemon
1 medium tomato, finely sliced
2 medium eggs
20g reduced-fat Cheddar, finely grated
salt and freshly ground black pepper, to taste

Level up your breakfast game with this herby twist on a morning staple. A super-simple addition to your morning routine, we've used everyone's favourite gadget to fry the egg directly onto the bagel, then come up with a creamy pesto topping that perfectly complements gooey, soft or hard yolks – the choice is yours. A dash of lemon juice ties everything together, adding a bright and citrusy tang to your toasted sandwich.

Line the basket of the air fryer with non-stick baking paper. Add the bagel, cut-side up. Air-fry at 180°C for 4 minutes until lightly toasted.

In a bowl, combine the pesto, cream cheese, basil and lemon juice. Mix well.

Spread the pesto mixture evenly onto the two bagel halves. Top with the sliced tomato. Crack an egg into the centre of each bagel half, then season to taste with salt and pepper and sprinkle over the cheese.

Cook for a further 8 minutes. The cheese should be melted and turning golden and the egg white set and cooked. Serve.

VEGGIE

DAIRY FREE

USE DF YOGHURT AND MILK

EASY TO HALVE

SEE INDEX

CLOUD PANCAKES

⏱ **20 MINS + 15 MINS FREEZING**   🍳 **8 MINS**   ✕ **SERVES 4**

PER SERVING:
168 KCAL / 31G CARBS

SPECIAL EQUIPMENT:
Electric hand whisk,
8 silicone muffin cases

2 egg whites
1 egg yolk
30g fat-free Greek yoghurt
50ml skimmed milk
1 tsp vanilla extract
60g plain flour
2 tbsp granulated sweetener
2 tbsp caster sugar
low-calorie cooking spray
2 tsp icing sugar
160g strawberries, sliced
100g raspberries
80g blueberries
4 tsp maple syrup

There's a reason these are called Cloud Pancakes – inspired by soft Japanese souffle-style pancakes, they're fluffy, bouncy... and probably as close to what you can imagine biting into a cottony cloud is actually like. Less like your typical crêpes or American pancakes and more like a sponge cake, they're certainly an exciting addition to your breakfast rotation. We've served them with strawberries, raspberries and blueberries, but you could even add whipped cream and chocolate sauce to make it a dessert.

Add the egg whites to a bowl and place into the freezer for 15 minutes.

Place the egg yolk, yoghurt, milk and vanilla into a bowl and whisk with an electric hand whisk on high speed for 2 minutes. The yolk mixture should be pale and thickened.

Sift the flour into the yolk mixture and whisk again on high speed for 1 minute. Place the bowl into the freezer.

Remove the egg whites from the freezer and whisk again on high speed for 2 minutes. The egg whites should be thick and hold stiff peaks.

Add the sweetener and caster sugar, one tablespoon at a time and whisk until fully mixed in between additions. The egg whites should be stiff and glossy and you should not be able to feel any grittiness in the mixture as the sugar should be dissolved. If it hasn't fully dissolved, continue to whisk for another minute.

For this recipe, the air fryer needs to be hot before cooking the pancakes. Spray the air fryer drawer with low-calorie cooking spray, then heat the air fryer at 170°C for 4 minutes. If you don't have a drawer in your air fryer, you will need to use a tin that fits inside instead.

Remove the egg yolk mixture from the freezer and spoon a third of the egg whites into the bowl. Gently fold in, trying not to knock out the air but folding until fully combined. Repeat with the remaining egg whites, adding in thirds until all the mixture is combined.

Spray the silicone muffin cases with low-calorie cooking spray and divide the mixture between the cases. Gently tap to flatten the mixture on top.

Place the cases into the air fryer and air-fry for 4 minutes. Gently loosen around the edge of the cases and tip directly into the drawer or tin. Cook for a further 4 minutes. The pancakes should be lightly golden and cooked through.

Remove from the air fryer, dust with icing sugar and serve two pancakes per person topped with the strawberries, raspberries, blueberries and a drizzle of maple syrup.

USE GF PASTRY

MAPLE PECAN PLAIT

⏱ **15 MINS + 20 MINS CHILLING**   🍳 **10–12 MINS**   ✕ **SERVES 12**

PER SERVING:
186 KCAL /18G CARBS

SPECIAL EQUIPMENT:
Food processor

100g pecans
3 tbsp brown granulated sweetener (use white if you prefer)
3 tbsp maple carob syrup
¼ tsp ground cinnamon
½ tsp vanilla extract
320g ready-rolled light puff pastry sheet
1 medium egg, beaten

FOR THE TOP:
1 tbsp icing sugar
2 tsp water
pinch of ground cinnamon
15g pecans, roughly chopped

TIP:
Once cool, freeze in a suitable container. Defrost overnight in the fridge. They can be enjoyed cold, or you can warm them in the oven to keep crisp.

When it comes to baked goods, you can't go wrong with a Danish pastry – but it doesn't always slot into your healthy lifestyle. That's why we've come up with a recipe that's half the calorie content of your average supermarket pastry. Armed with your food processor and your air fryer, you can make a delicacy to be enjoyed with a cup of tea. Because who doesn't love a sweet treat with their morning cuppa?

To make the filling, add the pecans to a food processor and blitz until very finely chopped.

Add the pecans to a mixing bowl along with the sweetener, maple syrup, cinnamon and vanilla. Mix until fully combined. The mixture should be quite sticky with a thick, paste-like consistency.

Unroll the pastry, leaving it on the paper backing. Slice it lengthways into four even strips. Using a teaspoon, spread the filling down the very centre of each strip (do not spread it out too far). Using a sharp knife, cut horizontal 'slits' all the way down each side of the filling, 1.5cm (⅝in) apart, aiming to keep each in line with the opposite side.

Brush the pastry with the beaten egg, either side of the pecan filling. Starting on the left, fold the first cut edge over the filling, then fold the opposite edge over, pressing down on the overlap. Repeat all the way to the end to create a long plait. Cut the plait into three and place each one onto a baking tray or plate lined with non-stick baking paper.

Repeat the plaiting process with the remaining three sections of pastry. You should now have 12 pastry plaits. Chill in the fridge for 20 minutes.

Line the air fryer basket with non-stick baking paper. Place the plaits into the baskets. (You may need to cook in batches depending on the size of your air fryer.) Brush with the remaining egg and air-fry at 170°C for 10–12 minutes, flipping over halfway through. They should be crisp and golden brown. Cook the remaining plaits, if needed.

Meanwhile, combine the icing sugar, water and cinnamon in a small bowl. Once cooked, brush each pastry with a little of the icing and sprinkle over the chopped pecans. Serve!

VEGGIE

VEGAN
USE VEGAN CHOCOLATE CHIPS

DAIRY FREE
USE DF CHOCOLATE CHIPS

GLUTEN FREE
USE GF BREAD

PEANUT BUTTER *and* BANANA TOAST

5 MINS   8 MINS   SERVES 2

PER SERVING:
341 KCAL /40G CARBS

2 slices wholemeal sourdough
2 tbsp peanut butter (crunchy or smooth, depending on your preference)
2 small bananas, peeled and thinly sliced
2 tsp maple syrup
10g chocolate chips

Let your tastebuds experience the best of both worlds with this sweet and salty breakfast delight. Simple to make, all it takes is a generous spread of your favourite nutritious peanut butter (crunchy or smooth, the choice is yours!) on a slice of bread. We used sourdough, but you're welcome to go with whatever your heart desires. Top it off with sliced bananas, maple syrup and chocolate chips, air-fry for just under 10 minutes – and voila!

Spread the sourdough with the peanut butter.

Arrange the banana slices over the top and drizzle with the maple syrup.

Sprinkle the chocolate chips over the top.

Air-fry at 180°C for around 8 minutes, until the sourdough is crisp and the banana is soft and golden brown around the edges.

Slice in half and serve.

RED PEPPER EGG BITES

 10 MINS  22 MINS  SERVES 12

PER SERVING:
87 KCAL /1.6G CARBS

SPECIAL EQUIPMENT:
Food processor, 12 silicone muffin cases or ramekins

low-calorie cooking spray
1 red pepper, deseeded and finely diced
80g baby spinach
100g reduced-fat vegetarian feta cheese
8 large eggs
250g fat-free cottage cheese
½ tsp onion granules
a good pinch of dried oregano
salt and freshly ground black pepper, to taste

Skip the morning trip to the coffee shop and make a batch of these protein-packed egg bites instead. Just whizz up your eggs and cottage cheese, pack with sweet red peppers and crumbly, tangy feta and let your air fryer do the rest. Keep them in the fridge, and you have a filling, grab-and-go breakfast that will keep you satisfied until lunchtime. It'll even save you a few pennies, too.

Spray a frying pan with low-calorie cooking spray and place over a medium to high heat. Add the red peppers and fry for 4–5 minutes, until lightly charred. Divide the red pepper between the muffin cases.

Return the pan to a lower heat. Add the spinach and stir for a minute or two until wilted.

Wrap the spinach in some paper towel or a clean kitchen towel and squeeze out any excess moisture. Roughly chop and add to the muffin cases. Crumble the feta on top.

Crack the eggs into a food processor, add the cottage cheese, onion granules and salt and pepper. Blitz until smooth and no white specks remain. If the mix looks grainy, blitz some more. This will ensure you have a smooth and creamy egg bite.

Cook in two batches. Pour the egg mixture into the muffin cases and use the end of a spoon to gently swirl the mixture together with the filling. You might find it easier to place these in the air fryer basket before you pour the egg mixture in. Sprinkle the oregano on top.

Air-fry at 160°C for 12–14 minutes until the egg bites are set and firm and golden on top.

Allow to cool slightly, then remove the egg bites from the muffin cases and serve warm, or cool completely and store in a container in the fridge to eat chilled.

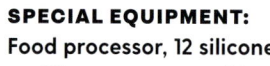

TIPS:
To freeze, wrap individually and freeze in an airtight container.

If using ceramic ramekins, you will need to spray with a little low-calorie cooking spray before filling.

FAKEAWAYS

FREEZE ME
BURGERS ONLY

BATCH COOK

GLUTEN FREE
USE GF ROLLS

HIGH PROTEIN

EASY TO HALVE
SEE INDEX

RANCH BURGERS

 **10 MINS**    **10 MINS**    **SERVES 4**

PER SERVING:
396 KCAL / 42G CARBS

250g 5%-fat beef mince
1 tsp garlic granules
1 tsp onion granules
½ tsp mixed herbs
½ tsp ground cumin
½ tsp mustard powder
low-calorie cooking spray
1 onion, peeled and sliced
salt and freshly ground black pepper, to taste

FOR THE RANCH SAUCE:
3 tbsp fat-free Greek yoghurt
2 tbsp lighter-than-light mayonnaise
1 tbsp finely chopped fresh chives
1 tbsp finely chopped fresh parsley
¼ tsp Dijon mustard
1 tsp lemon juice

TO SERVE:
4 brioche rolls, approx. 65g each, halved
4 reduced-fat cheese slices
100g gherkins, sliced
1 tomato, sliced
100g lettuce, sliced

Have you tried making burgers in your air fryer yet? Fakeaway night just got tastier with these juicy smash-style beef burgers on the menu. They're packed with air-fried caramelized onions, reduced-fat melted cheese and our homemade creamy herby ranch sauce. All nestled in a soft brioche roll with crispy lettuce, tomato and gherkins. Ready in just 20 minutes, it's one of those dinners you'll crave when you want something properly delicious without the faff!

In a bowl, combine the beef mince, garlic granules, onion granules, mixed herbs, cumin and mustard powder and season to taste with salt and pepper. Mix well with your hands until fully combined.

Divide the mixture into four and roll into balls. Place a sheet of non-stick baking paper onto your work surface and place the meatballs on top. Fold the paper over and press each meatball with your hand or the bottom of a glass until flattened and 1–2cm (½–¾in) thick.

Remove the basket from your air fryer and spray the drawer with low-calorie cooking spray. Alternatively, use a silicone liner or tin that fits inside your air fryer basket. Place the burgers and onions into the drawer. Depending on the size of your air fryer, you may need to do this in batches.

Air-fry for 10 minutes at 180°C, flipping the burgers over halfway through.

While the burgers and onions are cooking, make the ranch sauce. In a bowl, combine the yoghurt, mayonnaise, chives, parsley, mustard and lemon juice, then mix well. Season to taste with salt and pepper.

Spread a little of the ranch sauce onto the bottom of each roll. Place the burgers on the bottom half of the rolls, adding a slice of cheese, some cooked onions, gherkins, tomato and lettuce. Top with the other half of the rolls and serve.

CRISPY CAULIFLOWER TACOS

⏱ 30 MINS   12 MINS   ✕ SERVES 4

PER SERVING:
478 KCAL /59G CARBS

SPECIAL EQUIPMENT:
Mini chopper or blender

FOR THE PINK PICKLED ONIONS:
1 red onion, peeled and thinly sliced into rings
50ml white wine vinegar
1 tsp granulated sweetener (or sugar)
salt and freshly ground black pepper, to taste

FOR THE CHEESY SLAW:
150g fat-free Greek yoghurt
100g reduced-fat Cheddar, finely grated
1 tsp English mustard
2–3 tbsp cold water
175g white cabbage, finely shredded
1 carrot, grated (no need to peel)
2 spring onions, finely sliced

FOR THE TACOS:
2 tbsp self-raising flour
1 tsp garlic granules
1–2 tsp chilli powder
1 tsp ground cumin
1 tsp onion granules
75ml skimmed milk
1 cauliflower, cut into bite-size florets (about 450g prepared cauliflower)
low-calorie cooking spray
10g panko breadcrumbs
8 mini wraps
a bag of mixed leaves

These veggie tacos are a flavour explosion that'll bring the fiesta to your kitchen! We've coated cauliflower florets in a spiced batter, air-fried them until they're golden and crunchy, then served them up in soft mini wraps. Piled high with a creamy, cheesy slaw and sweet, tangy, pink pickled onions, they're bold, colourful and just the right amount of spicy. You won't miss the meat, trust us!

First, make the pink pickled onions. Place the onions, white wine vinegar, sweetener and some salt and pepper in a small bowl and mix well. Cover and refrigerate.

Next, make the cheesy slaw. Place the yoghurt, Cheddar and mustard in a blender or mini chopper and blitz until smooth. Add a little water to thin it down to a coating consistency. Place the cabbage, carrots and spring onions in a mixing bowl, add the dressing and stir until well combined. Season with salt and pepper, to taste. Cover and place in the fridge.

For the tacos, start by making the batter for the crispy cauliflower. Mix the flour, garlic granules, chilli powder, cumin, onion granules and some salt and pepper together in a small bowl. Whisk in the milk, until you have a smooth batter.

Place the cauliflower in a large bowl and drizzle the batter over, tossing the florets around as you pour, to ensure they are well coated.

Spray the air fryer basket with low-calorie cooking spray and add the cauliflower in a single layer. (You may need to do this in two batches or drawers, depending on the size of your air fryer.) Sprinkle the panko breadcrumbs over the top and spray with low-calorie cooking spray.

Air-fry at 200°C for 10–12 minutes, shaking halfway through, until the cauliflower is crisp on the outside and tender, but with bite in the centre.

Warm the wraps through in the microwave for a minute or two.

To assemble, top the wraps with mixed leaves, cheesy slaw, the crispy cauliflower and add a few pickled onions on top. Fold over and tuck in!

FREEZE COD AND SAUCE SEPARATELY

KATSU COD

 20 MINS  25 MINS  SERVES 4

PER SERVING:
273 KCAL / 35G CARBS

SPECIAL EQUIPMENT:
Stick blender

low-calorie cooking spray
1 medium onion, peeled and diced
3 garlic cloves, peeled and crushed
2 medium carrots, peeled and sliced
250g potato, peeled and chopped
1 tbsp garam masala
1 tbsp mild curry powder
1 tbsp soy sauce
½ tbsp garlic granules
½ tbsp onion granules
350ml vegetable stock (1 vegetable stock cube dissolved in 350ml boiling water)
2 tbsp cornflour
1 medium egg, beaten
50g panko breadcrumbs
350g skinless, boneless cod fillets
1 tbsp white granulated sweetener
salt and freshly ground black pepper, to taste

TO SERVE:
½ carrot, peeled and cut into ribbons
5g fresh coriander leaves

TO ACCOMPANY:
125g cooked basmati rice (+ 173 kcal per serving)

TIP:
Blend the sauce for twice as long as you think – you want the sauce to be super-smooth.

Chippy tea… but make it Japanese-inspired. If your chip shop order is fish and chips with a side of curry sauce, then this katsu cod curry is the dish for you. A light and flavoursome twist on a traditional Japanese meal, it's a good one for when your tastebuds are feeling adventurous – but your energy levels aren't. It preps in just 20 minutes – and then you can let your air fryer take over. It's tastier than a chippy tea – and a fraction of the calories!

Spray a saucepan with low-calorie cooking spray and set over a medium heat. Add the onion and garlic and gently fry for 4–5 minutes.

Add the carrots, potato, garam masala, curry powder, soy sauce, garlic granules, onion granules and stock to the pan and bring to the boil. Cover with a lid and reduce the heat. Simmer for 25–30 minutes until the potato and carrot are soft and cooked through. Stir occasionally.

Add the cornflour to a plate and season with salt and pepper. Add the egg and panko to two separate plates.

Slice the cod into chunky strips. Dip each piece of fish in the cornflour, then the egg, and finally the breadcrumbs.

Place the fish pieces into the air fryer basket and spray each one with low-calorie cooking spray. Air-fry at 170°C for 10–12 minutes until golden brown.

Once the potato and carrot for the sauce have cooked through, add the sweetener and use a stick blender to blitz the sauce until smooth. If your katsu sauce is too thick, add a splash of water; if too thin, simmer for a little longer.

Serve the cod with the sauce, garnished with carrot ribbons and coriander leaves.

CHICKEN and COCONUT CURRY

 10 MINS   **30 MINS** ✕ **SERVES 4**

PER SERVING:
280 KCAL /11G CARBS

400g chicken breast, diced
1 onion, peeled and diced
1 red pepper, sliced
100g fine green beans, trimmed
low-calorie cooking spray
2.5cm (1in) piece of root ginger, peeled and grated
4 garlic cloves, peeled and crushed
80g mild curry paste (we used korma)
2 tbsp tomato puree
1 x 400ml tin light coconut milk
juice of ½ lime
handful of fresh coriander leaves, roughly chopped
salt and freshly ground black pepper, to taste

TO ACCOMPANY:
125g cooked basmati and wild rice (+ 173 kcal per serving)

It doesn't get much simpler than this curry – and since it's only mild in flavour, it's bound to be a hit with the whole family. To save on time, we've mixed a ready-made curry paste with tomato puree – spiked with a hint of garlic and ginger for the gentlest of kicks. The coconut milk makes the sauce light and creamy, while your trusty air fryer keeps the chicken juicy and veggies fresh.

Remove the basket from the air fryer, and cook directly in the drawer, or use a silicone liner or cake tin that will fit in your air fryer.

Add the chicken, onion, pepper and green beans to the air fryer. Spray with low-calorie cooking spray and air-fry at 180°C for 5 minutes. Stir in the ginger and garlic and air-fry for a further 5 minutes.

Whisk together the curry paste, tomato puree and coconut milk until smooth. Stir into the chicken and veggies. Increase the temperature to 200°C and air-fry for a further 15–20 minutes, stirring halfway through, until the chicken is cooked through and the sauce is piping hot and slightly thickened.

Squeeze in the lime juice, add the coriander, season with salt and pepper, to taste, and serve!

TIP:
We used korma paste for a mild, fragrant curry, but you can use a spicier curry paste if you prefer.

SEE INDEX

CHICKEN *and* LEMON NOODLES

⏱ **10 MINS**   🍳 **25 MINS**   ✕ **SERVES 4**

PER SERVING:
313 KCAL / 39G CARBS

2 tbsp cornflour
1 tsp garlic granules
1 tsp onion granules
400g chicken breast, cut into chunky strips
low-calorie cooking spray
2 garlic cloves, peeled and crushed
2 tbsp soy sauce
1 tbsp honey
2 tbsp granulated sweetener
juice of 2 lemons
¼ tsp ground ginger
150g dried egg noodles
80g broccoli, cut into small florets
80g mangetout, sliced in half lengthways
2 spring onions, finely sliced
2 tsp sesame seeds
salt and freshly ground black pepper, to taste

Fancy a Chinese takeaway? Put that menu down and pick up your air fryer (not literally!). Light and refreshing, these Chicken and Lemon Noodles hit the spot when you're craving salty goodness – and the recipe takes just under half an hour to cook, so it's even faster than ordering in. Swap the veg out for your favourites, if you feel like it, but trust us when we say the spring onions are a non-negotiable!

Add the cornflour, garlic granules and onion granules to a bowl, season to taste with salt and pepper and mix well.

Drag the chicken strips through the cornflour mixture to give a light coating on all sides.

Remove the basket from your air fryer and spray the drawer with low-calorie cooking spray. Alternatively, use a silicone liner or tin that fits inside your air fryer basket. Add the coated chicken strips to the lined air fryer. Air-fry at 180°C for 5 minutes.

Meanwhile, add the crushed garlic, soy sauce, honey, sweetener, lemon juice and ginger to a bowl and mix well.

Pour the sauce into the air fryer and mix to coat the chicken, then continue to cook for 15 minutes.

Prepare the egg noodles according to the packet instructions (usually 4 minutes in a pan of boiling water). Drain and keep warm.

Add the broccoli and mangetout to the air fryer and cook for 5 minutes, then add the cooked noodles and stir to combine. Serve sprinkled with spring onions and sesame seeds.

DAIRY FREE

GLUTEN FREE
USE GF SOY SAUCE

LOW CARB

HIGH PROTEIN

ASIAN-STYLE FISH PARCELS

 15 MINS   **12 MINS**   ✗ **SERVES 2**

PER SERVING:
127 KCAL / 8G CARBS

2 x 100g skinless, boneless firm white fish fillets, such as haddock, cod, sea bass
1 carrot, peeled and cut into matchsticks
½ courgette, cut into matchsticks
2 spring onions, cut into matchsticks
1 pak choi, thickly shredded
handful of fresh coriander, chopped
1 tbsp dark soy sauce
2cm (¾in) piece of root ginger, peeled and grated
juice of ½ lime
1 garlic clove, peeled and crushed
½ red chilli, deseeded and chopped
pinch of granulated sweetener

TO ACCOMPANY:
125g cooked basmati rice (+ 173 kcal per serving)

A recipe you can unwrap? Consider this dish our gift to you! We've packed these delicious fish parcels with plenty of colourful and tasty veg, and cooked them in fragrant East Asian-inspired flavours like soy sauce, coriander, chilli and lime – they're a real treat for the senses. Serve each individual parcel at the table so you can watch your guests open them up and inhale the heavenly aromas.

Cut out two 50 x 37cm (20 x 14½in) rectangles of non-stick baking paper. Fold in half across the width to make a centre crease.

Open out and place one fish fillet on one half of each paper sheet.

In a large bowl, mix together the carrot, courgette, spring onions, pak choi and coriander.

In a separate bowl, mix together the soy sauce, ginger, lime juice, garlic, chilli and sweetener, until the sweetener has dissolved. Pour over the vegetable mixture and stir.

Divide the vegetable mixture between the two parcels and place on top of the fish.

Fold the non-stick baking paper sheets over the fish and vegetables and make small, tight folds around the edges to make two semi-circular 'pasty'-shaped parcels.

Carefully place the parcels in the air fryer basket (use a fish slice to help) and air-fry at 200°C for 10–12 minutes, depending on how thick your fish is.

Transfer each parcel to a plate using a fish slice. Open the parcels at the table and eat at once.

MEXICAN-STYLE FISH FINGER SANDWICH

 **20 MINS**  **6 MINS**  **SERVES 4**

PER SERVING:
454 KCAL / 52G CARBS

SPECIAL EQUIPMENT:
Mini chopper or blender

FOR THE GUACAMOLE:
1 small avocado
¼ cucumber, deseeded and grated
juice of ½ lime
½ tsp garlic granules
a few fresh coriander leaves, chopped
salt and freshly ground black pepper, to taste

FOR THE FISH FINGERS:
2 x 120g basa fillets, or any firm white fish, such as cod, haddock or pollock
1 tbsp plain flour
1 egg, beaten
60g tortilla chips, crushed into fine crumbs
½ tsp ground cumin
½–1 tsp chilli powder, mild or hot depending on your taste
low-calorie cooking spray

TO SERVE:
4 x 80g ciabatta rolls, cut in half
1 little gem lettuce, shredded

TO ACCOMPANY:
75g mixed salad (+ 15 kcal per serving)

TIP:
For a spicier sandwich, use chilli-flavour tortilla chips.

The humble fish finger butty is a firm favourite in our kitchen, so much so, we thought we'd put a new spin on it. Enter: our Mexican-style Fish Finger Sandwich. We've taken one of the nation's favourite comfort foods and added a Latin American twist – coating strips of basa fish in crushed tortilla chips, seasoning them with chilli (we'll leave the spice rating to you), and layering in a crispy ciabatta before coating in a cooling layer of guacamole.

First, make the guacamole. Cut the avocado in half, remove the stone and scoop the flesh into a mini chopper or blender. Add the grated cucumber, lime juice and garlic granules and blitz for a few seconds. Alternatively, mash together with a fork for a rougher texture. Stir through the coriander and season with some salt and pepper. Cover and refrigerate until needed.

Next, prepare the fish fingers. Use some paper towel to pat the fish dry and cut each fillet into six strips.

Arrange the flour, egg and tortilla crumbs in separate bowls. Stir the cumin and chilli powder into the tortilla crumbs. Season the flour with some salt and pepper.

Take each fish strip and coat lightly in flour, then dip in the egg and finally coat in tortilla crumbs, pressing lightly to make sure they stick.

Lay the fish fingers in the air fryer basket, leaving a small gap between each. Spray well with low-calorie cooking spray. Air-fry at 200°C for 6 minutes, until the crumbs are crisp and the fish is opaque all the way though.

Fill the ciabatta rolls with shredded lettuce, place three fish fingers into each, and top with the guacamole. Serve with a mixed salad.

BIRYANI-STYLE TURKEY

🕐 **10 MINS**   🍲 **25 MINS**   ✕ **SERVES 4**

PER SERVING:
461 KCAL / 56G CARBS

- low-calorie cooking spray
- 4 whole cloves
- 1 cinnamon stick
- 4 cardamom pods
- 1 medium onion, peeled and finely diced
- 4 garlic cloves, peeled and crushed
- 1 tsp garlic granules
- 1 tsp ground cumin
- 1 tsp ground coriander
- 1 tsp chilli powder
- 1 tsp paprika
- 2 tsp garam masala
- ½ tsp ground turmeric
- ½ tsp ground ginger
- 350g 2%-fat turkey mince
- 100g frozen peas
- 2 x 250g pre-cooked microwaveable rice pouches, or 500g cooked rice
- 100g fat-free Greek yoghurt
- 1 tbsp mango chutney
- 40g pumpkin seeds
- 40g dried cranberries
- salt and freshly ground black pepper, to taste

How can you not love a fragrant, one-pot, biryani-style dish that's ready in just 35 minutes? We've used turkey mince and a gorgeous blend of warming spices to create this crowd-pleasing fakeaway – all baked together in your air-fryer drawer. As it cooks, the rice soaks up every last bit of those lovely aromatic flavours, while the turkey remains wonderfully tender. We love topping ours with pumpkin seeds and dried cranberries for a lovely, sweet crunch. Make a big batch, and tomorrow's tea is already sorted!

Remove the basket from your air fryer and spray the drawer with low-calorie cooking spray. Alternatively, use a silicone liner or tin that fits inside your air fryer basket. Add the cloves, cinnamon, cardamom, onion and garlic and air-fry at 180°C for 5 minutes.

Add the garlic granules, cumin, coriander, chilli powder, paprika, garam masala, turmeric and ginger and mix well, then add the turkey mince and cook for 10 minutes, stirring occasionally to break up the large pieces of turkey mince.

Add the peas and rice and stir well. Cook for a further 10 minutes until the rice and peas are heated through and the turkey is cooked.

Meanwhile, add the yoghurt and mango chutney to a bowl and mix well.

Remove the cloves, cinnamon and cardamom pods from the rice. Sprinkle over the pumpkin seeds and cranberries and season to taste with salt and pepper. Serve with a drizzle of the mango yoghurt.

SWEET and SOUR CRISPY TOFU

⏱ **15 MINS**   🍲 **15 MINS**   ✕ **SERVES 4**

PER SERVING:
309 KCAL /27G CARBS

450g extra-firm tofu, cut into cubes
low-calorie cooking spray
1 tsp garlic granules
1 tsp onion granules
1 tsp smoked paprika
2 tbsp cornflour
1 red onion, peeled and sliced
2 peppers, deseeded and sliced
1 medium carrot, peeled and cut into strips
3 garlic cloves, peeled and crushed
100ml pineapple or orange juice
3 tbsp reduced-sugar-and-salt ketchup
2 tbsp soy sauce (light or dark)
2 tbsp granulated sweetener
2 tbsp rice vinegar
1 tbsp cornflour mixed to a slurry with 1 tbsp cold water
145g fresh pineapple, chopped into chunks
100g sugar snap peas, cut in half
2 spring onions, finely sliced
1 tsp sesame seeds (optional)
salt and freshly ground black pepper, to taste

TO ACCOMPANY:
125g cooked basmati rice (+ 173 kcal per serving)

If you love a takeaway treat, then we have a feeling this recipe will be a new fave for your Friday nights. Made to mimic your go-to Chinese restaurant order, this sweet-and-sour recipe has all the flavour of the classic dish without the grease. And because you're cooking it at home and sourcing all your own ingredients, it saves on cost as well as calories.

Pat the tofu cubes dry with paper towels. Add to a bowl and spray with low-calorie cooking spray. Sprinkle over the garlic granules, onion granules and paprika and toss to coat.

Add the cornflour and toss again to coat on all sides. Season to taste with salt and pepper.

If you have a dual-drawer air fryer, add the tofu to one basket and add the onion, peppers, carrot and garlic to the other. Spray with low-calorie cooking spray and cook at 200°C for 15 minutes. If you have a single basket, divide the tofu and veg on separate sides to prevent the tofu becoming soggy. Add the pineapple and sugar snap peas to the vegetables 5 minutes before the end of cooking.

Meanwhile, in a small saucepan, combine the pineapple or orange juice, ketchup, soy sauce, sweetener, rice vinegar and cornflour mixture. Heat on low for 10 minutes until thickened and glossy.

Remove the cooked tofu and vegetables from the air fryer, combine in a bowl and stir. Pour over the sticky sauce and mix to coat.

Sprinkle over the spring onions and sesame seeds and serve with rice or noodles.

TIP:
This is best served right away so the tofu stays crisp.

DAIRY FREE
USE DF YOGHURT

GLUTEN FREE
USE GF SOY SAUCE AND GF PITTA BREADS

HIGH PROTEIN

CHILLI BEEF KOFTA

🕐 **10 MINS**   🍳 **13-15 MINS**   ✕ **SERVES 2**

Swap your Friday night takeaway for a fakeaway feast with our Chilli Beef Kofta. This Turkish-inspired recipe calls for simple ingredients, and the whole thing comes together in under half an hour! Get stuck in with your hands to coat the beef in the spice mix, then skewer your sausage-shaped creations and stick them in your air fryer basket. While they cook, prepare your pittas – ready to top with the salad and sauce.

PER SERVING:
476 KCAL / 54G CARBS

FOR THE KOFTA:
250g 5%-fat beef mince
1 red chilli, deseeded and finely diced
1 tsp garlic granules
1 tsp onion granules
½ tsp smoked paprika
½ tsp ground cumin
½ tsp mild chilli powder
salt and freshly ground black pepper, to taste
low-calorie cooking spray

FOR THE GLAZE:
1 tbsp honey
¼ tsp garlic granules
¼ tsp chilli flakes

TO SERVE:
2 wholemeal pitta breads
100g salad leaves
4 cherry tomatoes, quartered
20g cucumber, sliced and halved
4 tbsp fat-free Greek yoghurt
1 tsp sweet chilli sauce

Add all the kofta ingredients, except the cooking spray, to a bowl and season to taste with salt and pepper. Mix well with your hands.

Divide the mixture into four and form into a sausage shape around a skewer.

Spray the air fryer with low-calorie cooking spray and add the kofta. Spray again and air-fry at 180°C for 5 minutes.

Now make the glaze. In a small bowl, combine the honey, garlic granules and chilli flakes. After 5 minutes of cooking, brush the kofta with the glaze. Cook for a further 8–10 minutes, brushing with the glaze and turning a few times throughout the cooking to get an even coating.

Lightly toast the pitta breads and layer up with salad leaves, tomatoes and cucumber. In a small bowl, combine the yoghurt with the sweet chilli sauce.

Remove the kofta kebabs from the air fryer and place on top of the salad, then drizzle over the yoghurt and serve.

BEEF and MUSHROOM CHOW MEIN

🕐 **15 MINS + 30 MINS MARINATING**   🍲 **15 MINS**   ✕ **SERVES 2**

PER SERVING:
420 KCAL /47G CARBS

2 garlic cloves, peeled and crushed
2cm (¾in) piece of root ginger, peeled and grated
1 tsp sesame oil
1 tbsp soy sauce
1 tsp rice vinegar
175g lean stir-fry beef strips
150g small mushrooms, quartered
150g beansprouts
4 spring onions, trimmed and sliced
1 pak choi, shredded
½ red pepper, thinly sliced
2 x 50g egg noodle nests

FOR THE SAUCE:
1 tsp sesame oil
1 tbsp mirin
1 tbsp soy sauce
1 tbsp oyster sauce

Sometimes, Friday rolls around and there's nothing you want more than to pop in an order at your local takeaway. We've come up with this recipe so you can satisfy your cravings without letting all your hard work go to waste. Garlic, ginger, sesame oil, soy sauce and rice vinegar combine to create those mouthwatering authentic flavours – and because you can just stick it in the air fryer, it's almost as fuss-free as ordering in.

Place the garlic, ginger, sesame oil, soy sauce and rice vinegar in a bowl and mix well.

Add the steak strips and stir around until well coated. Cover and leave to marinate in the fridge for 30 minutes.

Remove the basket from the air fryer and add the steak. Air-fry at 200°C for 6 minutes.

Stir in the vegetables (reserve a few spring onions for garnish) and air-fry for another 6 minutes, stirring halfway through.

While the chow mein cooks, prepare the egg noodles according to the packet instructions (usually 4 minutes in a pan of boiling water). Drain and keep warm.

Mix the sauce ingredients together, then add to the air fryer, along with the egg noodles. Air-fry for a further 2–3 minutes until thoroughly warmed through. Serve!

CRISPY LAMB

🕐 25 MINS   🍲 20 MINS   ✕ SERVES 4

PER SERVING:
494 KCAL / 63G CARBS

- 1 tsp ground cumin
- 1 tsp garlic granules
- 1 tsp smoked paprika
- ½ tsp ground cinnamon
- ¼ tsp ground turmeric
- 2 tbsp cornflour
- 1 medium egg
- 400g lean lamb steaks, cut into thin strips
- low-calorie cooking spray
- 125g uncooked basmati rice
- 1 small red onion, peeled and sliced
- 1 red pepper, deseeded and sliced
- 1 large carrot, peeled and cut into matchsticks
- ½ courgette, cut into batons
- juice of 1 large orange
- 1 tbsp pomegranate molasses
- 1 tbsp runny honey
- 1 tbsp balsamic vinegar
- 1 x 400g tin chickpeas, drained and rinsed
- 80g pomegranate seeds
- salt and freshly ground black pepper, to taste
- small handful of fresh parsley, chopped

Been eyeing up our Crispy Chilli Beef recipe but not a fan of the heat? This Crispy Lamb is the perfect alternative. A Moroccan-inspired recipe with fragrant flavours, tender lamb is cut into strips and coated in a lightly spiced batter that's packed with flavour. Simply pop the strips into your air fryer until they're deliciously crisp. Coated in an orange and pomegranate sauce and served with fluffy rice that can be rustled up while the lamb cooks, you can tick off all the food groups with little hassle.

Remove the basket from the air fryer or line it with non-stick baking paper.

Add the cumin, garlic granules, paprika, cinnamon and turmeric to a mixing bowl. Add the cornflour, then season with salt and pepper. Stir until well combined.

Crack the egg into a bowl and beat. Add the lamb strips and mix around until well coated with the egg.

Remove the lamb strips from the egg, allowing excess egg to drain. Add the lamb to the bowl of seasoned cornflour and toss to coat. The egg and cornflour will form a light batter on the lamb.

Add the lamb strips to the air fryer and spray well with low-calorie cooking spray. Air-fry at 200°C for 20 minutes until crispy.

Meanwhile, cook the rice. Rinse the rice under cold running water. Add to a pan with 200ml salted water. Bring to the boil, then reduce the heat to low. Cover and cook for 10 minutes.

Now prepare the sauce. Spray a frying pan with low-calorie cooking spray and place over a medium to high heat. Add the onion, pepper, carrot and courgette and stir-fry for 5 minutes.

Add the orange juice, pomegranate molasses, honey and balsamic vinegar to a small bowl and whisk together. Add to the frying pan and allow to bubble for 5 minutes until it thickens.

When the rice has been cooking for 10 minutes, stir in the drained chickpeas. Cover and cook for a further 5 minutes, then turn off the heat and leave covered.

When the lamb is cooked, remove from the air fryer and stir into the sauce.

Fluff up the chickpea rice with a fork and stir through the pomegranate seeds. Serve topped with the crispy lamb, with the parsley sprinkled over.

USE GF BUNS

SEE INDEX

PORK *and* PARMESAN BURGERS

🕐 **10 MINS**   🍲 **16 MINS**   ✕ **SERVES 4**

PER SERVING:
385 KCAL / 30G CARBS

low-calorie cooking spray
1 small red onion, peeled and finely chopped
2 garlic cloves, peeled and crushed
1 tsp finely chopped fresh rosemary
400g 5%-fat pork mince
30g Parmesan, finely grated
100g lighter-than-light mayonnaise
juice of ½ lemon
salt and freshly ground black pepper, to taste

TO SERVE:
4 x 60g wholemeal rolls
¼ iceberg lettuce, shredded
2 tomatoes, sliced

TO ACCOMPANY:
75g mixed salad (+ 15 kcal per serving)

TIPS:
You can substitute the pork mince for turkey mince, if you prefer.

To freeze, once shaped into burgers, place a piece of non-stick baking paper in between each, wrap well and freeze. Defrost, reshape and cook as per instructions.

For when you're bored of beef or just fancy something different, these juicy pork burgers are a tasty alternative to your standard cheeseburger. We've kept them tender with red onion and Parmesan, and added a little garlic and rosemary to give them an Italian flair. Talk about chef's kiss! Even better – the salty, nutty flavour of the Parmesan means these burgers need minimal extra flavouring, keeping the calories and fat down even more!

Spray a frying pan with low-calorie cooking spray and place over a medium heat. Add the chopped onion and fry for 5 minutes, until soft. Add the garlic and rosemary and cook for a minute. Allow to cool.

Place the pork mince in a bowl with the cooked onion and Parmesan. Mix until well combined. Season with salt and pepper, if needed. You can test the seasoning by cooking off a penny-sized piece in a frying pan, and adjust the seasoning to taste.

Divide the mixture into four and shape into burgers.

Spray the air fryer basket with a little low-calorie cooking spray, add the burgers and air-fry at 200°C for 10 minutes, carefully flipping halfway through.

Meanwhile, mix the mayonnaise with the lemon juice and season with some salt and pepper.

When the burgers are cooked through and no pink remains, split the rolls in half and fill with the lettuce and tomato slices. Add the burgers and top with lemon mayonnaise. Serve!

FAKEAWAYS

USE DF YOGHURT

USE GF BREADCRUMBS

SEE INDEX

KEFTEDES (CYPRIOT-STYLE MEATBALLS)

 15 MINS   18 MINS   SERVES 4

PER SERVING:
267 KCAL / 12G CARBS

120g potato, raw and unpeeled, grated
500g 5%-fat minced pork
½ red onion, peeled and finely chopped
2 garlic cloves, peeled and crushed
1 tsp ground cinnamon
large handful of flat-leafed parsley, chopped
20g panko breadcrumbs
1 medium egg, beaten
juice of ½ lemon
½ tsp salt
½ tsp coarsely ground black pepper
2 tsp extra virgin olive oil, for brushing the meatballs
lemon wedges, to serve

TO ACCOMPANY:
50g fat-free Greek yoghurt (+ 58 kcal per serving)

Keftedes are a Cypriot meatball. Traditionally, they're deep-fried to make them crisp and brown – but to keep the calories down, we've just brushed them with olive oil and cooked them in a non-traditional air fryer! Made from veal, pork, or sometimes half pork, half beef, they're usually rugby-ball shaped (but we won't be inspecting yours, don't worry!). We've gone for extra-lean pork to keep the calories down even more. Red onions and garlic add even more flavour, while grated potato creates a moist and fluffy texture.

Wrap the grated potato in a clean kitchen towel, hold over the sink and squeeze out any excess water.

Place the potato in a bowl with the remaining meatball ingredients, except the olive oil and lemon wedges, and use your hands to thoroughly mix.

Divide into 12 evenly sized pieces. Shape into oval 'rugby balls'.

Brush the bottom of the air fryer basket with olive oil, then use the rest to brush all sides of the keftedes. Place in the air fryer basket and air-fry at 200°C for 10 minutes. Carefully flip if you can and continue air-frying for a further 6–8 minutes, until the keftedes are well browned with crisp edges.

Serve with Greek yoghurt and lemon wedges, for squeezing.

TIP:
If the keftedes feel like they have stuck to the basket at the halfway point, don't struggle to flip them as you will risk them falling apart. Leave them until the end of cooking time and carefully remove from the basket with a palette knife or fish slice.

USE DF CHEESE AND YOGHURT

USE GF WRAPS

SEE INDEX

FAJITA CRUNCHWRAP

 15 MINS   32 MINS   ✗ SERVES 4

PER SERVING:
328 KCAL /27G CARBS

low-calorie cooking spray
300g chicken breast, diced
1 pepper (any colour), deseeded and sliced
1 red onion, peeled and sliced
2 tsp garlic granules
1 tsp ground coriander
1 tsp ground cumin
1 tsp oregano
½ tsp mild chilli powder
2 tbsp tomato puree
2 tbsp water
4 soft tortilla wraps, approx. 40g per wrap
60g reduced-fat Cheddar, finely grated
salt and freshly ground black pepper, to taste
lime wedges, to serve

FOR THE CREAMY SALSA:
120g cherry tomatoes, diced
2 spring onions, sliced
10g fresh coriander, chopped
juice of 1 lime
3 tbsp fat-free Greek yoghurt

TO ACCOMPANY:
75g mixed salad (+ 15 kcal per serving)

Step away from the takeaway menu and make this Mexican-inspired fakeaway instead! These wraps are packed with tender chicken and colourful peppers, coated in our punchy fajita spice mix, then parcelled up and crisped to perfection in your air fryer. The creamy salsa and grated cheese give them a gooey, rich centre that's lower in calories than you might think. Make a big batch and pop the extras in the freezer. They're brilliant for a quick, high-protein lunch when you don't have time to cook.

Remove the basket from your air fryer and spray the drawer with low-calorie cooking spray. Alternatively, use a silicone liner or tin that fits inside your air fryer basket.

Add the chicken, pepper and onion to the lined basket. Sprinkle over the garlic, coriander, cumin, oregano and chilli powder and toss to coat. Season to taste with salt and pepper. Spray with low-calorie cooking spray and air-fry at 180°C for 20 minutes. The chicken should be cooked through and the vegetables soft.

Add the tomato puree and water and mix well. Air-fry for a further 1–2 minutes.

Meanwhile, make the creamy salsa by adding the tomatoes, spring onion, coriander, lime juice and yoghurt to a small bowl. Mix and season to taste with salt and pepper.

Divide the chicken mixture between the wraps. Add the grated cheese and creamy salsa on top. Starting at the top, fold the sides of the wrap over the chicken to create a hexagon-shaped parcel.

Place into the air fryer, seam-side down, and air-fry at 180°C for 5–10 minutes, turning over halfway through. The wrap should be crisp and turning golden brown.

SPANISH-STYLE CHICKEN *and* BUTTER BEAN RICE

🕐 **10 MINS**   🍲 **25 MINS**   ✕ **SERVES 4**

DAIRY FREE

GLUTEN FREE
USE GF STOCK CUBES AND CHORIZO

HIGH PROTEIN

EASY TO HALVE
SEE INDEX

PER SERVING:
476 KCAL / 46G CARBS

75g chorizo, diced
1 small onion, peeled and finely chopped
500g chicken breast, diced
4 garlic cloves, peeled and crushed
2 tsp smoked sweet paprika
1 x 400g tin butter beans, rinsed and drained
juice of 1 lemon
100ml chicken stock (1 chicken stock cube dissolved in 100ml boiling water)
100g fine green beans, trimmed and cut in half
2 x 250g microwaveable long-grain rice pouches
salt and freshly ground black pepper, to taste
handful of fresh parsley, chopped, to garnish
lemon wedges, to serve

Who doesn't love a dish that takes you straight to your favourite holiday spot? Life's a beach with this easy-peasy rice dish that draws inspiration from a paella made by a Spanish friend many moons ago! It's simple – just juicy chicken, creamy butter beans, fresh green beans, and a generous squeeze of zesty lemon. You won't find us claiming you can cook up a true paella in your air fryer, but with just a few swaps, we've re-created those sunny Spanish flavours.

Depending on your style of air fryer, remove the basket from the drawer or insert a silicone liner or cake tin.

Add the chorizo and onion to the air fryer and air-fry at 180°C for 5 minutes.

Meanwhile, place the chicken in a bowl and coat the pieces with the garlic and smoked paprika and season well with salt and pepper.

Add the chicken to the air fryer and stir into the chorizo and onion. Air-fry at 180°C for 8 minutes.

Add the butter beans, lemon juice and stock and stir well. Lay the green beans on top (don't stir in).

Increase the temperature to 200°C and air-fry for 5 minutes.

Squeeze the rice pouches to separate the grains and add to the air fryer, stirring well to make sure everything is well mixed and the rice is coated with the spices and stock.

Air-fry at 200°C for a final 6 minutes, stirring halfway through.

Ensure the rice is piping hot and serve garnished with parsley and lemon wedges for squeezing.

FAKEAWAYS

DAIRY FREE
USE DF CHEESE AND YOGHURT

GLUTEN FREE
USE GF WRAPS

HIGH PROTEIN

EASY TO HALVE
SEE INDEX

TEX-MEX TACOS

🕐 10 MINS    30 MINS   ✕ SERVES 4

PER SERVING:
407 KCAL / 36G CARBS

low-calorie cooking spray
1 medium red onion, peeled and sliced
1 pepper (any colour), deseeded and sliced
3 garlic cloves, peeled and crushed
250g 5%-fat beef mince
2 tbsp smoked paprika
1 tsp ground cumin
1 tsp ground coriander
1 tsp garlic granules
1 tsp onion granules
1 tsp dried oregano
½ tsp chilli powder
150g passata
2 tbsp tomato puree
1 tsp granulated sweetener
100g tinned black beans, drained and rinsed
salt and freshly ground black pepper, to taste

TO SERVE:
½ red onion, peeled and finely sliced
3 tbsp rice vinegar
4 soft tortilla wraps, approx. 40g per wrap
100g reduced-fat Cheddar, finely grated
100g fat-free Greek yoghurt
juice of 1 lime
120g cherry tomatoes, diced
5g fresh coriander, chopped

TO ACCOMPANY:
75g mixed salad (+ 15 kcal per serving)

Let us introduce you to Tex-Mex tacos, made in your air fryer! It's an easy Mexican-inspired fakeaway feast of rich tomato-coated beef mince with peppers and black beans, all nestled in crispy tortilla wraps and topped with pickled red onion and a yoghurt drizzle. The best part? Everything cooks in your air fryer drawer, so you'll have minimal washing up. It's a proper win-win!

Remove the basket from your air fryer and spray the drawer with low-calorie cooking spray. Alternatively, use a silicone liner or tin that fits inside your air fryer basket. Add the onion, pepper and garlic and air-fry at 180°C for 5 minutes.

Add the beef mince and sprinkle over the paprika, cumin, coriander, garlic granules, onion granules, oregano and chilli powder. Mix to coat. Cook for 10 minutes, stirring occasionally to break up any large pieces of the beef mince.

While the mince cooks, combine the ½ red onion with the rice vinegar in a small bowl, mix and leave to one side.

Add the passata, tomato puree, sweetener, black beans and salt and pepper to the air fryer. Mix again and continue to cook for 5 minutes, until the beef is cooked and the sauce has thickened.

Divide the beef mixture between the tortilla wraps, spreading it onto the bottom half of each wrap. Sprinkle over the cheese and fold over the top half of each wrap, pressing down flat. You should now have four semi-circle taco shapes.

Spray the wraps with a little low-calorie cooking spray and air-fry for a further 5–10 minutes until lightly golden, crispy, and the cheese has melted. You may need to do this in batches.

Mix the yoghurt with the lime juice. Serve each taco with some of the pickled red onion, chopped tomatoes, lime yoghurt and a sprinkle of coriander.

HOISIN PORK *with* NOODLES

⏱ **15 MINS**   🍲 **16 MINS**   ✕ **SERVES 4**

PER SERVING:
450 KCAL / 50G CARBS

500g 5%-fat pork mince
6 spring onions, trimmed and sliced
2 tsp sesame oil
4cm (1½in) piece of root ginger, peeled and grated
2 garlic cloves, peeled and crushed
1 tsp Chinese 5-spice
1 carrot, peeled and cut into matchsticks
1 red pepper, deseeded and diced
200g dried egg noodles
100g hoisin sauce
2 tbsp soy sauce
juice of ½ lime

Ready in minutes with minimal faff, this air-fryer fakeaway is an easy-peasy weeknight wonder the whole family will love. This tasty dish combines tender, low-fat pork mince with garlic, punchy ginger and crunchy veg. There are no hidden nasties or hard-to-find ingredients. Once the noodles are cooked, you'll simply stir through sweet and salty hoisin sauce, soy sauce and lime juice. Trust us, you're going to be adding this to your meal plan on repeat. It'll have you wondering why you ever ordered takeaway!

Remove the basket from the air fryer drawer, or use a silicone liner or cake tin that fits inside the drawer.

Add the pork, spring onions (reserve some green parts for garnish), 1 teaspoon of the sesame oil, the ginger, garlic and 5-spice and mix well. Air-fry at 200°C for 8 minutes, stirring and breaking up any large clumps.

Toss the vegetables in the remaining sesame oil and add to the air fryer, but don't stir them into the pork mince yet. Air-fry for a further 5 minutes.

While the vegetables cook, cook the noodles according to the packet instructions – usually 4 minutes in a pan of boiling water. Drain well, then add to the air fryer with the hoisin sauce, soy sauce and lime juice, stir well and air-fry for a final 2–3 minutes.

Sprinkle over the reserved spring onions and serve.

MOROCCAN-STYLE TOFU KEBABS

 **20 MINS**  **20-25 MINS**  **SERVES 4**

PER SERVING:
212 KCAL /25G CARBS

SPECIAL EQUIPMENT:
Food processor

150g firm tofu
120g tinned chickpeas, drained and rinsed
½ red onion, peeled and finely diced
½ red pepper, deseeded and finely diced
1 tsp smoked paprika
1 tsp garlic granules
½ tsp ground cumin
½ tsp ground coriander
½ tsp ground turmeric
½ tsp mild chilli powder
80g plain flour
salt and freshly ground black pepper, to taste
low-calorie cooking spray
4 tbsp fat-free Greek yoghurt
1 tbsp finely chopped fresh mint, plus a handful of mint leaves, to serve

TO ACCOMPANY:
75g mixed salad
   (+ 15 kcal per serving)
30g tortilla wrap
   (+ 85 kcal per serving)

Packed with tofu, chickpeas, onion and peppers, these Moroccan-style kebabs are rich in protein and flavour. One of the main reasons they're so tasty is down to the spongy, fluffy texture of the tofu, which soaks up the flavours of the fragrant Middle Eastern spices. Blended to fuse everything together, it's super simple and extra tasty! The creamy mint yoghurt on the side perfectly offsets the spices, cooling you down in between bites.

Slice the tofu in half and place the pieces between a clean kitchen towel or paper towel. Gently press on the tofu using a large pan or tins to remove the moisture. You may need to do this a few times to ensure the tofu looks dry and firm.

Add the chickpeas to a food processor and pulse to a roughly mashed consistency. Alternatively, you can mash the chickpeas well with a fork.

Crumble the pressed tofu into a large mixing bowl, then add the chickpeas, onion and pepper, and mix.

Add the paprika, garlic granules, cumin, coriander, turmeric and chilli powder and season to taste with salt and pepper. Mix well. Add the flour and mix again.

Divide the mixture into eight pieces and shape each using your hands into an oblong kofta-type shape.

Line the air fryer basket with non-stick baking paper and place the kebabs onto the paper. Spray with low-calorie cooking spray and air-fry at 180°C for 20–25 minutes, turning over halfway through. The outside should be dry and crispy and the kebab holding its shape when lightly pressed.

While the kebabs cook, combine the yoghurt and mint in a small bowl. Serve alongside the kebabs with an accompaniment of your choice. We think this works great with a tortilla wrap or flatbread and salad.

MAPLE and BACON MEATBALLS

 15 MINS    **25 MINS**   **SERVES 4**

PER SERVING:
306 KCAL / 19G CARBS

4 smoked bacon medallions, cut into small dice
4 tsp maple syrup
low-calorie cooking spray
400g 5%-fat pork mince
1 tsp garlic granules
1 tsp paprika
20g panko breadcrumbs
2 tbsp milk
1 egg yolk
½ tsp salt
freshly ground black pepper, to taste

FOR THE SAUCE:
500g passata
1 tsp garlic granules
1 tbsp maple syrup
salt and freshly ground black pepper, to taste

TO ACCOMPANY:
125g cooked spaghetti
(+ 174 kcal per serving)

Smoky pork meatballs with sticky toffee sweetness... these bold meatballs are a midweek treat for sure! We've used light and nutty maple syrup to caramelize bacon and pork meatballs, then smothered the results in a maple-infused tomato sauce. Simple, store-cupboard ingredients for an adventurous dish! And ready in less than half an hour, what's not to love?

Toss the bacon pieces in a teaspoon of maple syrup and spray with low-calorie cooking spray. Remove the basket from the air fryer or insert a cake tin or silicone liner. Add the bacon and air-fry at 200°C for 8 minutes, stirring halfway through, until the bacon is caramelized and crispy.

While the bacon cooks, make the meatballs. Add the pork, garlic granules, paprika, panko, milk, egg yolk and salt and pepper to a bowl and use your hands to thoroughly mix together. Divide into 24 even-sized pieces and roll into balls.

When the bacon is cooked, add the meatballs, drizzle with 3 teaspoons of maple syrup and air-fry the bacon and meatballs at 200°C for 4 minutes.

While the meatballs cook, prepare the sauce. Mix the passata with the garlic granules and maple syrup. Season with salt and pepper to taste.

Stir the sauce through the meatballs, and air-fry for 10–12 minutes, stirring halfway through. The meatballs are cooked when the sauce is bubbling, and the tops of the meatballs are caramelized.

Serve over spaghetti.

TIP:
You can use whatever milk you have in your fridge, including plant-based milks.

SRIRACHA SALMON with ROASTED PINEAPPLE SALSA

⏱ **10 MINS + 30 MINS MARINATING**   🍲 **25 MINS**   ✕ **SERVES 4**

PER SERVING:
321 KCAL /16G CARBS

1 tbsp sriracha
1 tbsp honey
juice of 1 lime
½ tsp garlic granules
4 x 110g skinless salmon fillets
300g fresh pineapple, peeled and cut into 1.5cm (⅝in) slices
1 red pepper, cut in half and deseeded
low-calorie cooking spray
4 spring onions, trimmed and sliced
handful of fresh coriander leaves, chopped
salt and freshly ground black pepper, to taste

TO ACCOMPANY:
125g cooked basmati rice (+ 173 kcal per serving)

This sweet and spicy salmon dish is a total flavour bomb, and the air fryer makes it even easier to make! We've marinated skinless salmon fillets in a punchy mix of sriracha, honey and lime, then crisped them up until caramelized around the edges and flaky in the middle. Paired with a zingy, roasted pineapple salsa, it's the perfect fakeaway treat that's light, juicy and bursting with colour.

Mix together the sriracha, honey, a squeeze of the lime juice and the garlic granules in a bowl. Add the salmon fillets and mix until well coated. Cover and refrigerate for 30 minutes while you prepare the salsa.

Spray the pineapple and red pepper with low-calorie cooking spray and season both with salt and pepper.

Place the pepper into the air fryer basket, cut-side down. Add the pineapple and air-fry at 200°C for 12–15 minutes. The pineapple should be caramelized and the pepper charred, but still firm. Remove from the air fryer and leave for 10 minutes to cool.

When the pineapple and pepper have cooled enough to handle, cut around and discard the woody pineapple core. Cut the pineapple and pepper into 5mm (¼in) dice. Add to a bowl with the spring onions, coriander and the remaining lime juice and stir well. Cover and pop into the fridge while you cook the salmon.

Lay the salmon fillets into the air fryer basket and air-fry at 200°C for 8–10 minutes, until golden and caramelized around the edges and opaque through the centre.

Serve with the pineapple salsa.

TIP:
This is excellent served with rice, or vegetables for a lighter option.

DAIRY FREE
USE DF YOGHURT SUBSTITUTE

GLUTEN FREE
USE GF NAAN BREAD

HIGH PROTEIN

EASY TO HALVE
SEE INDEX

SPICY BEEF and CHICKPEA FLATBREAD

 **20 MINS**    **10 MINS**    **SERVES 4**

PER SERVING:
425 KCAL /53G CARBS

SPECIAL EQUIPMENT:
Mini chopper or blender

250g 5%-fat minced beef
1 tsp garam masala
1 tsp garlic granules
1 tsp onion granules
½ tsp ground cumin
½ tsp ground coriander
½ tsp ground ginger
½ tsp salt
low-calorie cooking spray
1 x 400g tin chickpeas, drained and rinsed

FOR THE MANGO RAITA:
½ ripe mango, diced
125g fat-free Greek yoghurt
½ tsp garlic granules
1 tbsp lime juice
½ red chilli, finely chopped
small handful of fresh mint leaves, chopped
salt and freshly ground black pepper, to taste

TO SERVE:
4 mini naan breads, approx. 65g each
1 little gem lettuce, shredded
2 tomatoes, diced
¼ cucumber, diced
½ red onion, peeled and sliced
handful of fresh coriander, chopped

This easy-to-assemble flatbread is one of those dishes that'll have friends and family hounding you for the recipe – you've been warned! We've taken mini naans and topped them with spicy minced beef and roasted chickpeas, with a refreshing mango raita drizzled over the top. Clocking in at 30 minutes in total to make from start to finish, it's a fab lazy yet flavoursome dinner – and if you want to save yourself even more time, you can cheat with shop-bought tzatziki instead of homemade raita. Your secret's safe with us!

Place the mince in a bowl and add the garam masala, garlic granules, onion granules, cumin, coriander and ginger. Don't add the salt until just before cooking. Mix until well combined. Cover and leave to the side for the flavours to infuse while you prepare the mango raita.

Place the mango, yoghurt, garlic granules and lime juice in a mini chopper or blender and blitz until smooth. Stir in the chilli and mint and season with salt and pepper. Cover and refrigerate until needed.

Season the spiced mince with the salt. Remove the basket from the air fryer and spray inside with low-calorie cooking spray. Add the seasoned mince and use a spoon to break it into chunks. Air-fry at 200°C for 3 minutes.

Break the mince up again and stir in the chickpeas. Air-fry at 200°C for a further 5–7 minutes, stirring halfway through.

While the mince cooks, warm the naans, either in a toaster, microwave, or if you have a dual-drawer air fryer, pop them in there for 3 minutes.

Pile the salad on the naan, top with the spicy beef and chickpeas and drizzle with the mango raita. Sprinkle over the coriander. Serve!

FAKEAWAYS

USE GF PASTRY

SEE INDEX

CHICKEN CURRY STRUDEL

 15 MINS  **13 MINS** ✕ **SERVES 4**

PER SERVING:
449 KCAL /44G CARBS

200g cooked chicken breast, cut into small pieces
2 spring onions, trimmed and finely sliced
75g half-fat crème fraîche
1½ tbsp mild curry paste (we used korma)
1 tsp mango chutney
320g ready-rolled light puff pastry sheet
1 tbsp milk
½ tsp black onion seeds
salt and freshly ground black pepper, to taste

TO ACCOMPANY:
75g mixed salad (+ 15 kcal per serving)

It doesn't get much more comforting than a classic curry or warm strudel. So what about... a savoury curry strudel? Get a load of this creamy coronation-style chicken curry, wrapped in crisp flaky pastry and baked to perfection in your air fryer – no oven necessary! This recipe makes four servings, but if you're someone who needs a whole batch of curry pasties on hand (we know we are), you can always double up and stash a load in your freezer.

Place the chicken breast and spring onions in a mixing bowl. Add the crème fraîche, curry paste and mango chutney. Mix well, taste and season with salt and pepper if required.

Unroll the chilled pastry in front of you, keeping it on the non-stick baking paper to make it easier to handle. Use a sharp knife to cut it in half lengthways then widthways, giving you four equal rectangles.

Divide the filling into four and spread a portion down the short side of each pastry rectangle, leaving a 1cm (½in) space around the edges, and the other half free. Use a sharp knife to cut slits into the other half of the pastry. Brush the edges with milk, then fold the pastry over to encase the filling and crimp the edges together to seal. Brush the tops with milk and then sprinkle the black onion seeds over the top.

Line the air fryer basket with non-stick baking paper and add the strudels. Air-fry at 200°C for 10 minutes. Carefully flip and air-fry for a further 3 minutes to crisp the underside. Serve!

TIP:
To freeze the strudels, once cool, wrap individually and freeze in an airtight container. Defrost and reheat for a few minutes in the air fryer or oven to keep crisp.

BAKES AND ROASTS

USE DF YOGHURT

SEE INDEX

CHICKEN and MANGO CHUTNEY TRAYBAKE

 15 MINS   **30 MINS** ✕ **SERVES 4**

PER SERVING:
428 KCAL /49G CARBS

500g chicken breast, diced
low-calorie cooking spray
1 red onion, peeled and sliced
1 red pepper, deseeded and sliced
100g courgette, cut into batons
2 tbsp curry powder
1 tbsp garlic granules
1 x 400g tin chickpeas, drained and rinsed
1 x 250g microwaveable rice pouch
4 tbsp mango chutney
juice of 1 lime
160g spinach
3 tbsp fat-free Greek yoghurt
salt and freshly ground pepper, to taste
10g fresh coriander, stalks and leaves, roughly chopped, to garnish

The beauty of this traybake is you can stick everything in your air fryer and skip the multi-pan clear up! Deliciously spiced chicken and a colourful array of vegetables are cooked until golden and juicy. Then just stir in the chickpea rice and sticky mango and lime sauce and you have a tasty, healthy, all-in-one meal within the hour!

Add the chicken directly to the air fryer drawer or use a silicone liner. Spray with a little low-calorie cooking spray. Air-fry at 180°C for 10 minutes.

Add the onion, pepper and courgette. Sprinkle over the curry powder and garlic granules and mix to coat. Cook for a further 10 minutes.

Add the chickpeas, rice, 3 tablespoons of the mango chutney and the lime juice. Mix well to combine and cook for another 5 minutes.

Add the spinach, mix in and cook for a final 5 minutes until wilted.

In a small bowl, combine the yoghurt with the remaining tablespoon of mango chutney and mix until smooth.

The chicken should be cooked through, the vegetables soft and the sauce sticky. Season to taste with salt and pepper, drizzle over the yoghurt, sprinkle over the coriander and serve.

FREEZE ME

BATCH COOK

DAIRY FREE
USE DF CHEESE AND SOURED CREAM

GLUTEN FREE

HIGH PROTEIN

EASY TO HALVE
SEE INDEX

CHILLI COTTAGE PIE JACKETS

🕐 **15 MINS**   🍲 **40 MINS**   ✕ **SERVES 4**

PER SERVING:
466 KCAL / 52G CARBS

4 baking potatoes, approx. 175g each
250g 5%-fat minced beef
1 medium onion, peeled and diced
1 pepper (any colour), deseeded and diced
1 carrot, peeled and diced
2 garlic cloves, peeled and crushed
1 x 400g tin chopped tomatoes
2 tbsp tomato puree
1 tbsp Henderson's relish
1 tsp garlic granules
1 tsp onion granules
1 tsp smoked paprika
1 tsp dried oregano
2 tsp mild chilli powder (or hot if you prefer)
½ tsp ground cumin
150ml boiling water
80g tinned kidney beans, drained and rinsed
80g tinned sweetcorn, drained
80g reduced-fat Cheddar, finely grated
4 tbsp reduced-fat soured cream
4 tsp finely sliced fresh chives (optional)
salt and freshly ground black pepper, to taste

TO ACCOMPANY *(optional)*:
75g mixed salad (+ 15 kcal per serving)

There's a reason we're all obsessed with jacket potatoes – they're comforting, easy to rustle up, and the topping possibilities are endless. For this recipe, we've hollowed out the potatoes to make room for our hearty, veggie-rich chilli filling – saving the potato flesh to pile on top with golden melty cheese. We've gone for beef mince, but it works just as well with pork or turkey. A perfect warmer when the evenings start to get a bit cooler.

Pierce the potatoes and cook for 5 minutes each in the microwave until soft.

Depending on the style of your air fryer, either remove the basket from your air fryer or use a silicone liner or tin that fits inside your air fryer. Place the beef mince into the drawer and air-fry at 200°C for 5 minutes.

Add the onion, pepper, carrot and garlic and cook for a further 8 minutes. The beef should be browned and the vegetables starting to soften.

Pour in the chopped tomatoes and add the tomato puree, Henderson's relish, garlic granules, onion granules, paprika, oregano, chilli powder, cumin, boiling water, kidney beans and sweetcorn and give it a good stir. Reduce the temperature and air-fry at 180°C for 12 minutes.

Meanwhile, scoop out the centres of the potatoes into a bowl (reserving the shells) and season to taste with salt and pepper. Mash until smooth.

Spoon the chilli into the potato shells and top each half with the mashed potato. Sprinkle over the cheese and place into the air fryer for 5–10 minutes until the cheese is bubbling and golden brown.

Serve with the soured cream and sprinkle over the chives, if using.

BAKES and ROASTS

VEGGIE
USE VEGETARIAN SAUSAGES

VEGAN
USE VEGAN SAUSAGES AND VEGAN CREAM CHEESE

GLUTEN FREE
USE GF SAUSAGES AND GNOCCHI

HIGH PROTEIN

EASY TO HALVE
SEE INDEX

CREAMY SAUSAGE GNOCCHI

⏲ **10 MINS**   **24 MINS**   ✕ **SERVES 4**

PER SERVING:
390 KCAL / 41G CARBS

340g low-fat chicken chipolatas
low-calorie cooking spray
100g reduced-fat cream cheese
50g sun-dried tomato paste
200ml water
1 tsp garlic granules
4 spring onions, trimmed and finely sliced
500g fresh gnocchi
small handful of fresh basil leaves, shredded
12 cherry tomatoes, halved
salt and freshly ground black pepper, to taste

TO ACCOMPANY *(optional)*:
75g mixed salad (+ 15 kcal per serving)

There really aren't many dishes cosier than a steaming bowl of gnocchi. We've made this one even cosier by tossing in tasty bites of low-fat sausage that add even more substance to these soft and chewy Italian dumplings. We've also popped in some fresh cherry tomatoes for a juicy burst of texture, not forgetting the basil garnish – a classic pairing for a reason!

Remove the basket from the air fryer or use a silicone liner inside your air fryer drawer.

Break or slice the sausages up into bite-size pieces and place in the air fryer. Spray with low-calorie cooking spray and air-fry at 180°C for 6 minutes.

While the sausage cooks, beat together the cream cheese, tomato paste, water and garlic granules. Season to taste with salt and pepper.

Add the spring onions and gnocchi to the sausages and stir well. Air-fry at 180°C for 10 minutes, shaking occasionally or stirring to ensure even cooking.

After 10 minutes, add the creamy tomato sauce and the basil, reserving a little for garnish, and stir well. Scatter the cherry tomatoes on top, but do not stir through. Air-fry at 180°C for a further 6–8 minutes, until the tomatoes are cooked and beginning to brown.

Stir and serve garnished with the remaining basil.

TIPS:

Gnocchi are small Italian dumplings, typically made from potato and wheat flour. They come in a range of varieties, such as cauliflower, pumpkin, spinach, tomato and even stuffed with mozzarella! These are all suitable for this recipe, but do check the nutrition info, as some can be higher in calories than regular gnocchi.

If using a silicone liner, you may need to increase the cooking time by a few minutes.

BAKES and ROASTS

BAKES and ROASTS

HAM and ASPARAGUS CHICKEN

⏱ **25 MINS**   🍲 **25 MINS**   ✕ **SERVES 4**

PER SERVING:
394 KCAL /20G CARBS

SPECIAL EQUIPMENT:
Mallet or rolling pin

4 skinless, boneless chicken breasts, approx. 150g each
2 garlic cloves, peeled and crushed
4 slices Parma ham, excess fat removed
4 reduced-fat cheese slices
120g asparagus spears
low-calorie cooking spray
salt and freshly ground black pepper, to taste

FOR THE CHEESE SAUCE:
400ml skimmed milk
3 tbsp cornflour, mixed to a slurry with 3 tbsp of the milk
pinch of mustard powder
80g reduced-fat Cheddar, finely grated

TO ACCOMPANY:
80g steamed vegetables (+ 38 kcal per serving)

TIP:
This recipe will fit in one single-drawer air fryer or use both drawers of a dual-drawer air fryer.

Two types of cheese and under 400 calories! These juicy chicken breast parcels are packed with salty Parma ham, melty cheese slices, and tender asparagus spears – then drizzled with a tasty light cheese sauce. The result is a comforting dish that works perfectly as a midweek meal when you're on the go. Just assemble them and let your air fryer take over!

Place the chicken breasts between two pieces of cling film or non-stick baking paper and bash with a meat mallet or rolling pin to make them as thin as possible.

Discard the cling film and lay the flattened chicken breasts out on a chopping board. Divide the garlic between the chicken breasts and rub over. Season well with salt and pepper. Place a slice of Parma ham on top of each chicken breast. Place a cheese slice on top of the Parma ham.

Divide the asparagus into four equal bunches and place a bunch on one end of each chicken breast. Roll each chicken breast up, starting at one end and enclosing the filling.

Remove the basket from your air fryer drawer. Place the rolled up chicken breasts, seam-side down, into the drawer. Alternatively, use a cake tin or a silicone liner.

Prepare the cheese sauce. Pour the milk into a saucepan and place over a medium heat until it is steaming hot and just about to boil. Stir the cornflour slurry into the hot milk, stirring or whisking constantly. Bring to the boil, then reduce the heat and simmer for a minute or two, stirring constantly, until thickened.

Remove from the heat and stir in the mustard powder and cheese, reserving a quarter of the cheese for topping. Season well with salt and pepper.

Pour the cheese sauce over the chicken but not the asparagus ends. Spray the asparagus ends with a little low-calorie spray. Sprinkle the top with the remaining grated cheese.

Air-fry at 170°C for 20 minutes, until the chicken is cooked, the asparagus is lightly charred and the cheese sauce topping is bubbling and golden brown.

BAKES and ROASTS

AUBERGINE PARMIGIANA

🕐 **10 MINS**   🍲 **25-30 MINS**   ✕ **SERVES 2**

PER SERVING:
383 KCAL /34G CARBS

2 aubergines, sliced lengthways to the thickness of a £1 coin
low-calorie cooking spray
2 x 400g tins chopped tomatoes
2 tbsp tomato puree
2 tsp granulated sweetener
2 tsp garlic granules
1 tsp dried sage
1 tbsp red wine vinegar
1 tbsp Henderson's relish
10 sprigs of fresh thyme, leaves removed
5g fresh basil, finely chopped
20g mozzarella, torn
30g Italian-style hard cheese, finely grated
30g wholemeal bread, made into breadcrumbs
20g pine nuts, finely chopped
salt and freshly ground black pepper, to taste

TO ACCOMPANY *(optional):*
75g mixed salad (+ 15 kcal per serving)

When you're craving comfort on a plate, our Aubergine Parmigiana has your back. A healthy take on an Italian-American classic, we've layered sliced aubergine coated in a rich and tangy tomato sauce and plenty of Italian seasoning, and finished things off with a mozzarella cheese breadcrumb topping. It's the perfect combination of veggie goodness and satisfying crispy crunch. And since the fresh herbs can be swapped out for dried, it can easily be turned into a store-cupboard essentials meal – simple to whip up, and ready in under an hour.

Place the slices of aubergine into the air fryer and spray with low-calorie cooking spray. Air-fry at 190°C for 8–10 minutes, turning halfway through until turning golden brown and softening. Remove from the air fryer and set aside.

In a bowl, combine the chopped tomatoes, tomato puree, sweetener, garlic, sage, vinegar, Henderson's, thyme and basil. Season to taste with salt and pepper.

Depending on your style of air fryer, add the tomatoes directly into the drawer or into a silicone liner. Air-fry at 180°C for 10 minutes, stirring occasionally.

Add the mozzarella, hard cheese, breadcrumbs and pine nuts to a small bowl and season to taste. Leave to one side.

Remove half of the tomatoes from the air fryer and add a layer of the cooked aubergine. Spoon the removed tomatoes back on top. Sprinkle over the breadcrumb mixture and air-fry for a further 5–10 minutes until melted and golden brown.

TIP:
You can swap the fresh thyme and basil for 2 teaspoons of dried, if you prefer.

VEGGIE

FREEZE ME
FREEZE WITHOUT THE BBQ SAUCE TOPPING

BATCH COOK

GLUTEN FREE
USE GF BBQ SAUCE

HIGH PROTEIN

EASY TO HALVE
SEE INDEX

SMOKY HALLOUMI *and* SWEET POTATO BAKE

🕒 **15 MINS**   🍲 **25 MINS**   ✕ **SERVES 4**

PER SERVING:
402 KCAL / 42G CARBS

225g block of reduced-fat halloumi, cut into 2cm (¾in) dice
500g sweet potatoes, peeled and cut into 2cm (¾in) dice
1 red onion, peeled and sliced
1 green pepper, deseeded and sliced
1 x 400g tin chickpeas, drained and rinsed
low-calorie cooking spray
2 tsp smoked paprika
1 tsp garlic granules
1 tsp dried oregano
10 cherry tomatoes, halved
100g BBQ sauce
salt and freshly ground black pepper, to taste

TO ACCOMPANY:
80g steamed veg (+ 38 kcal per serving)

Pairing halloumi with sweet potato might seem unusual, but stick with us on this one, and we promise you won't regret it. We've taken chunks of salty halloumi and coated them in a smoky paprika and garlic mix to add just the right amount of kick. The sweet potatoes combine with peppers, onions, and chickpeas to hit your protein and fibre goals, and the whole thing cooks in just 25 minutes in your air fryer. Don't forget the BBQ drizzle!

Place the halloumi, sweet potatoes, onion, pepper and chickpeas in a large mixing bowl. Spray well with low-calorie cooking spray, then sprinkle over the smoked paprika, garlic granules and oregano. Season with salt and pepper and toss around to evenly coat the veggies and halloumi.

Remove the basket from the air-fryer drawer, or line with a silicone liner. Add the sweet potato and halloumi mix. Air-fry at 180°C for 15 minutes, giving it a shake halfway through.

Add the tomatoes and shake the drawer. Air-fry for a further 5–10 minutes, until the sweet potato is tender and the halloumi is crisp.

Divide between four plates and drizzle with the BBQ sauce.

TIP:
This recipe will fit in one large air fryer drawer, or both drawers of a dual-drawer air fryer.

VEGGIE
USE VEGETARIAN FETA

VEGAN
USE DF PASTRY AND FETA-STYLE CHEESE

FREEZE ME

BATCH COOK

DAIRY FREE
USE DF PASTRY AND FETA-STYLE CHEESE

GLUTEN FREE
USE GF PASTRY

BEETROOT *and* FETA TART

⏱ **10 MINS**   🗑 **25 MINS**   ✕ **SERVES 2**

PER SERVING:
458 KCAL /55G CARBS

120g cooked beetroot (not pickled), sliced
1 red onion, peeled and sliced
1 tbsp balsamic vinegar
½ tsp garlic granules
½ tsp granulated sweetener
60g reduced-fat feta cheese
low-calorie cooking spray
150g ready-rolled light puff pastry sheet, cut into two 12 x 15cm (5 x 6in) rectangles
1 medium egg, beaten
salt and freshly ground black pepper, to taste

FOR THE TOP:
½ tsp balsamic vinegar
1 tsp honey

TO ACCOMPANY:
75g mixed salad (+ 15 kcal per serving)

This colourful beetroot tart is a dish that looks like it takes a long time to prepare, but is actually assembled in just over half an hour – an ideal option if you're hosting or are simply on the go. A simple and light puff pastry base is topped with vibrant beetroot, red onion and salty feta, it's tasty on the tongue and easy on the eye. We've finished it off with a sweet and tangy honey and balsamic drizzle to add even more flavour. Pair it with a side salad and serve warm or cold.

Line the air fryer basket with non-stick baking paper.

Add the beetroot and onion to a bowl. Add the balsamic, garlic granules and sweetener. Stir to coat and season to taste with salt and pepper.

Layer up the onion and beetroot into two sections on the baking paper, slightly smaller than the size of your puff pastry rectangles (12 x 15cm/5 x 6in). Crumble half of the feta over each section of vegetables. Spray with low-calorie cooking spray. Air-fry at 160°C for 10 minutes.

Add the puff pastry rectangles on top of each section of vegetables, pressing the edges down onto the baking paper. You can use your fingertips or press down with a fork.

Brush the top of the pastry with the egg and air-fry for a further 8–10 minutes until golden brown and crisp.

Lift the paper out and flip the tarts over, then crumble over the remaining feta. Return to the air fryer for 3–5 minutes.

Add the vinegar and honey to a small bowl and mix until smooth and combined.

Remove the tarts from the air fryer. The pastry should be crisp and the vegetables soft and turning brown around the edges. Drizzle over the honey and balsamic mixture and serve with salad or accompaniment of choice.

USE DF CREAM CHEESE

SEE INDEX

SUN-DRIED TOMATO CHICKEN BAKE

🕒 **15 MINS**   🍲 **35–40 MINS**   ✕ **SERVES 4**

PER SERVING:
409 KCAL / 29G CARBS

400g chicken breast, diced
1 tbsp garlic granules
1 tbsp onion granules
1 tbsp smoked paprika
1 tbsp dried oregano
2 tbsp red pesto
2 tbsp sun-dried tomato paste
1 tbsp tomato puree
150ml boiling water
1 red onion, peeled and finely sliced
1 red pepper, deseeded and finely sliced
400g white potatoes (no need to peel)
salt, for the cooking water
50g reduced-fat cream cheese
50g sun-dried tomatoes, sliced
low-calorie cooking spray

TO ACCOMPANY *(optional):*
80g steamed vegetables
   (+ 38 kcal per serving)

When you don't fancy juggling several different pans on the hob, this cosy chicken bake is your knight in a shining air fryer! We've diced tender chicken breast and added sun-dried tomato paste to give it a rich and herby relish. Golden-brown potato slices on top create a crisp texture that gives the dish a satisfying crunch. Did we mention the whole thing cooks in just under an hour? Complete your plate with a colourful helping of steamed veg on the side.

Add the chicken to a bowl. Add the garlic granules, onion granules, paprika, oregano, pesto, sun-dried tomato paste and tomato puree. Stir to combine. Depending on the style of your air fryer, either place the chicken into the drawer (after removing the basket) or place into a silicone liner. Air-fry at 180°C for 10 minutes.

Add the boiling water, red onion and sliced pepper. Cook for a further 10 minutes.

Meanwhile, slice the potatoes to about the thickness of a £1 coin. Add to a pan of cold, salted water and bring to the boil, then reduce the heat and simmer for 5–8 minutes until the potatoes are just softening.

Add the cream cheese and sun-dried tomatoes to the chicken mixture and mix until blended.

Add the potato slices to the top of the chicken, overlapping them slightly. Spray with a little low-calorie cooking spray and cook for 15–20 minutes until the potatoes are golden brown.

BAKES and ROASTS

BOLOGNESE POTATO HASH

⏱ **15 MINS**   🍲 **40 MINS**   ✕ **SERVES 4**

PER SERVING:
304 KCAL / 27G CARBS

500g 5%-fat beef mince
1 medium onion, peeled and finely diced
2 medium carrots, peeled and finely diced
2 celery sticks, finely diced
80g mushrooms, finely diced
2 garlic cloves, peeled and crushed
1 x 400g tin chopped tomatoes
2 tbsp tomato puree
1 tbsp Henderson's relish
1 tsp mixed herbs
1 tsp garlic granules
1 tsp onion granules
1 tsp granulated sweetener
150ml beef stock (1 beef stock cube dissolved in 150ml boiling water)
300g potatoes, peeled and cut into approx. 2cm (¾in) cubes
low-calorie cooking spray
salt and freshly ground black pepper, to taste

TO ACCOMPANY:
75g mixed salad (+ 15 kcal per serving)

It's universally agreed that potatoes make everything better, so why not add them to your spag bol? That's exactly what we've done with this Bolognese Potato Hash – a twist on a family classic, with spaghetti swapped out for crispy potato cubes. It's bound to become a firm favourite, and cooks in just under an hour from start to finish, making it a perfect new addition to your family meal rotation. Or you can freeze the leftovers and save it for a hassle-free lunch!

Depending on the style of your air fryer, either remove the basket from your air fryer or use a silicone liner or tin that fits inside your air fryer. Place the beef mince into the drawer and air-fry at 200°C for 5 minutes.

Add the onion, carrots, celery, mushrooms and garlic and cook for a further 8 minutes. The beef should be browned and the vegetables starting to soften.

Pour in the chopped tomatoes and add the tomato puree, Henderson's relish, mixed herbs, garlic granules, onion granules and sweetener. Add the beef stock and give it a good stir. Reduce the temperature and cook at 180°C for 12 minutes.

Meanwhile, add the potato cubes to a pan of cold salted water. Bring to the boil, then reduce the heat and simmer for 5–8 minutes until the potatoes are just softening.

Season the bolognese to taste. Drain the potatoes and add to the top of the bolognese. Spray with low-calorie cooking spray. Cook for 15 minutes until the potato cubes are golden brown.

PEA and HAM CROQUETTES

 30 MINS   40 MINS   SERVES 4

PER SERVING:
327 KCAL /49G CARBS

SPECIAL EQUIPMENT:
Potato masher

750g potatoes, peeled and cut into chunks
250g frozen peas
4 spring onions, trimmed and finely sliced
100g sliced ham, finely chopped
1 tsp garlic granules
1 tbsp green pesto
20g Parmesan, finely grated
45g panko breadcrumbs
low-calorie cooking spray
salt and freshly ground black pepper, to taste

TO ACCOMPANY:
75g mixed salad (+ 15 kcal per serving)

TIPS:
Serve three croquettes per person as a main meal for 327 calories.

Alternatively, serve two per person as a side dish for 216 calories.

There's something so comforting about the classic combination of pea and ham, and we've given it a crispy twist with these golden croquettes! Mashed potato, sweet peas and salty ham are all mixed with pesto and a sprinkle of Parmesan, then rolled in panko breadcrumbs for a light, crunchy finish in the air fryer. Serve three croquettes each with a side salad for a satisfying main, or two as a delicious alternative to chips or mash. Either way, they're guaranteed to be a hit!

Cook the potatoes in a pan of boiling, salted water for about 15 minutes, until a knife slides easily through the centre.

Add the peas and bring back to the boil for 3–4 minutes until the peas are cooked. Drain well and let sit for 5 minutes to air dry.

Mash the potatoes and peas together.

Add the spring onions, ham, garlic granules, pesto and Parmesan and mix well. Taste and season with salt and pepper, if needed.

Divide the mix into 12 even portions and roll each into a cylinder around 6cm (2½in) in length.

Place the panko breadcrumbs on a plate and roll each croquette around in the breadcrumbs until lightly coated.

Spray the air fryer basket with low-calorie cooking spray and add the croquettes, leaving a gap between each to ensure even cooking. Spray the croquettes with low-calorie cooking spray and air fry at 200°C for 16–18 minutes, carefully turning halfway through. You may need to do this in two batches, depending on the size of your air fryer.

Serve!

HUMMUS-CRUSTED CHICKEN

5 MINS **18–20 MINS** **SERVES 2**

PER SERVING:
254 KCAL / 5.9G CARBS

75g 30%-reduced-fat hummus
½ tsp ground cumin
½ tsp garlic granules
2 x 150g skinless, boneless chicken breasts
½ tsp toasted sesame seeds
lemon wedges, to serve

TO ACCOMPANY:
75g mixed salad (+ 15 kcal per serving)

Hummus-coated chicken? We know what you're thinking, but trust us when we say this is a classic case of 'Don't knock it 'til you've tried it.' Your favourite chickpea-based dip is actually a great way to jazz-up chicken breasts. As the hummus cooks, it forms a light golden crust that keeps the chicken moist while maximizing its flavour. We've thrown in some garlic and cumin to give your tastebuds an extra treat, and served it alongside some zingy lemon wedges that you can squeeze as you please.

Mix the hummus with the cumin and garlic granules together in a small bowl.

Smother the chicken breasts with the hummus and place in the air fryer basket. Sprinkle the tops with the sesame seeds.

Air-fry at 180°C for 18–20 minutes until the hummus is golden and the chicken is cooked through.

Serve with the lemon wedges on the side.

HARISSA MARMALADE SALMON

⏱ **10 MINS**   🍲 **25 MINS**   ✕ **SERVES 2**

PER SERVING:
461 KCAL /42G CARBS

1 red onion, peeled and sliced
2 medium carrots, peeled and cut into batons
low-calorie cooking spray
40g harissa paste
80g fine-cut marmalade
1 tsp dried thyme
1 tsp garlic granules
2 x 110g skinless salmon fillets
150g green beans, trimmed
salt and freshly ground black pepper, to taste

Harissa and salmon is about to be your new favourite combination. This recipe is super-light and – with the help of your trusty air fryer – ready in under half an hour. What's not to love? The sticky harissa and marmalade mixture we've rustled up gives the salmon fillets a fiery flavour – creating a glazed effect that adds to the natural sweetness of the fish. Cooked on a bed of onions, carrots and green beans, it's an all-in-one winner that will satisfy and save on washing-up!

Add the onion and carrots to the air fryer drawer, spray with low-calorie cooking spray and season to taste with salt and pepper. Air-fry at 190°C for 15 minutes.

In a small bowl, combine the harissa, marmalade, thyme and garlic and mix until smooth.

Place the salmon fillets on top of the vegetables and spoon half of the harissa mixture over the top. Cook for 5 minutes.

Spoon over the remaining harissa mixture, add the green beans and cook for a further 5 minutes. The salmon and vegetables should be cooked through and turning brown around the edges.

STEAK BITES and POTATOES

⏱ **10 MINS**   🍲 **40 MINS**   ✕ **SERVES 2**

PER SERVING:
427 KCAL /35G CARBS

400g baby potatoes, cut into even chunks
low-calorie cooking spray
a few sprigs of fresh thyme
150g trimmed green beans
75g reduced-fat cream cheese
100ml beef stock (½ beef stock cube dissolved in 100ml boiling water)
300g lean, thick-cut rump steak, cut into 2.5cm (1in) cubes
½ tsp onion granules
salt and freshly ground black pepper, to taste

We've cracked the code for the easiest and tastiest steak dinner! Think seasoned steak bites, crispy, golden potatoes and vibrant green beans. Your air fryer means you can forget about standing over a hot pan, all that washing-up and a smoky kitchen. While everything's sizzling away, knock up our lightning-fast pepper sauce and prepare for a seriously impressive dinner!

Put the potatoes in a pan of boiling salted water and cook for 15 minutes until just tender.

Drain well. Spray with low-calorie cooking spray and season well with salt and pepper. Toss around in the pan to coat.

Remove the basket from the air fryer and add the potatoes. Tuck the sprigs of thyme into the potatoes. Air-fry at 200°C for 10 minutes until the potatoes are starting to brown.

Spray the green beans with low-calorie cooking spray and season with salt and pepper.

When the potatoes have been cooking for 10 minutes, add the green beans to the top. Don't shake the basket at this point. Air-fry for a further 6 minutes.

While the beans and potatoes cook, whisk the cream cheese and stock together in a small pan. Add ½–1 teaspoon of freshly ground black pepper, place over a medium heat and allow to bubble until it thickens. Keep warm.

Season the steak cubes with the onion granules and some salt and pepper. Spray with low-calorie cooking spray.

When the potatoes and green beans have finished cooking, give the basket a good shake.

Add the steak bites to the top – do not shake!

Air-fry for 3–5 minutes, depending on how you like your steak. For medium, we cooked the steak bites for 3 minutes.

When the steak is cooked to your liking, serve with the pepper sauce on the side.

FREEZE COUSCOUS SEPARATELY

USE GF STOCK CUBE AND COUSCOUS

SEE INDEX

SUMAC CHICKEN with ROASTED VEGETABLES and HERBY COUSCOUS

⏱ 30 MINS + 45 MINS MARINATING   🍲 22 MINS   ✗ SERVES 4

PER SERVING:
425 KCAL / 46G CARBS

4 large skinless, boneless chicken thighs, approx. 150g each
1 red onion, peeled and cut into 1cm (½in) wedges
150g butternut squash, peeled and cut into 1cm (½in) fingers
1 red pepper, deseeded and sliced
1 courgette, cut into 1cm (½in) slices
2 garlic cloves, peeled and crushed
low-calorie cooking spray
1 lemon, cut into slices
salt and freshly ground black pepper, to taste

FOR THE MARINADE:
2 tbsp sumac
½ tsp chilli flakes
1 tsp ground cinnamon
1 tsp ground cumin
3 garlic cloves, peeled and crushed
juice of 1 lemon
2 tsp tomato puree

FOR THE HERBY COUSCOUS:
200g couscous
300ml chicken stock (½ chicken stock cube dissolved in 300ml boiling water)
½ tsp garlic granules
small handful of flat-leafed parsley, chopped
small handful of fresh mint leaves, chopped
juice of ½ lemon

Take a trip to the Middle East without even leaving your kitchen with this roasted vegetable traybake. Sumac is the star of the show here, and we've thrown plenty of other flavours in to quite literally spice things up! Serve with a colourful array of vegetables doused in lemon and garlic, alongside a fluffy herby couscous to soak up all the delicious spicy, lemony goodness.

Place the chicken thighs in a medium bowl with all the marinade ingredients. Mix well until evenly coated, cover and place in the fridge for 45 minutes.

Place the onion, butternut squash, red pepper, courgette and garlic in a bowl. Spray liberally with low-calorie cooking spray and season with salt and pepper. Toss the vegetables to coat them well.

Remove the basket from the air fryer drawer and scatter the vegetables straight into the bottom, in a single layer. Alternatively, use a silicone liner or cake tin that fits in your air fryer drawer.

Nestle the marinated chicken thighs into the vegetables, spacing them out evenly. Tuck the lemon slices into the chicken and vegetable mixture. Spray the chicken thighs and lemon slices with a little low-calorie cooking spray.

Air-fry at 180°C for 20–22 minutes until the chicken thighs are cooked, there is no pinkness and the juices run clear. The vegetables should be tender and be starting to blacken a little at the edges.

While the chicken and vegetables are roasting, make the herby couscous. Place the couscous in a medium bowl and pour over the boiling-hot chicken stock. Cover and leave to soak for 10 minutes, or according to the packet instructions, until all the stock has been absorbed.

TIP:
This recipe will fit in one large, single-drawer air fryer or use both drawers of a dual-drawer air fryer.

Stir the couscous with a fork to break up the grains. Stir in the garlic granules, parsley, mint and lemon juice. Season well with salt and black pepper, to taste.

Serve the hot roasted sumac chicken, vegetables and their juices with the herby couscous. You can freeze the chicken and couscous separately.

VEGGIE
USE VEGETARIAN SAUSAGES

VEGAN
USE VEGAN SAUSAGES AND SWAP HONEY FOR MAPLE SYRUP

FREEZE ME

DAIRY FREE

GLUTEN FREE
USE GF SAUSAGES

HIGH PROTEIN

EASY TO HALVE
SEE INDEX

SAUSAGE, SAGE *and* ROSEMARY TRAYBAKE

🕐 15 MINS   🍲 30–33 MINS   ✕ SERVES 4

PER SERVING:
423 KCAL / 37G CARBS

250g new potatoes, sliced
low-calorie cooking spray
1 medium red onion, peeled and sliced
150g courgette, sliced
8 reduced-fat pork sausages
1 tbsp dried sage
1 tbsp dried rosemary
1 tsp garlic granules
2 tbsp honey
50ml apple juice
1 x 400g tin butter beans, drained and rinsed
200g Tenderstem broccoli, trimmed

Get ready to fall in love with this one-pot wonder! This hearty sausage traybake combines juicy bangers with new potatoes and creamy butter beans, all coated in a sticky-sweet herby glaze. Thanks to your air fryer, the glaze caramelizes beautifully, and there's barely any washing-up to tackle after dinner! Perfect for those chilly weeknight evenings when you can't be bothered with a pile of pots and pans.

Place the potatoes directly into the air fryer drawer and spray with low-calorie cooking spray. Air-fry at 190°C for 5 minutes.

Add the onion, courgette and sausages to the air fryer and cook for a further 10 minutes.

In a small bowl, mix together the sage, rosemary, garlic, honey and apple juice. Pour over the sausages and vegetables and toss around to coat well. Cook for a further 10 minutes.

Add the beans and broccoli and cook for a final 5–8 minutes. The sausages should be cooked and the vegetables browned. Serve.

BAKES *and* ROASTS

VEGGIE
USE VEGETARIAN PESTO AND FETA

VEGAN
USE DF PESTO AND CHEESES

FREEZE ME

BATCH COOK

DAIRY FREE
USE DF PESTO AND CHEESES

GLUTEN FREE
USE GF PASTA

EASY TO HALVE
SEE INDEX

ROASTED VEGETABLE PASTA BAKE

🕐 **15 MINS**   🍲 **30–35 MINS**   ✕ **SERVES 4**

PER SERVING:
453 KCAL / 60G CARBS

SPECIAL EQUIPMENT:
Food processor or stick blender

2 peppers (any colour), deseeded and chopped
1 red onion, peeled and chopped
3 garlic cloves, peeled
300g courgette, chopped
80g mushrooms, halved
300g tomatoes, halved
160g butternut squash, peeled and cut into small chunks
2 tbsp red pesto
2 tsp dried basil
2 tsp garlic granules
low-calorie cooking spray
80g feta cheese, roughly crumbled
250g pasta (any shape you prefer)
50g reduced-fat Cheddar, finely grated
salt and freshly ground black pepper, to taste

Pasta bakes are good for the soul, especially this roasted vegetable number. We've packed it with an array of colourful veg so you are over halfway to your five-a-day in one dish, but feel free to swap out any of our choices for your personal favourites – you can even throw in some whole chillies for a fiery kick. Of course, we didn't forget the comforting cheesy goodness everyone loves – we've mixed some crumbly feta into the sauce. Bake in your air fryer until the cheese is gooey and bubbling, then tuck in!

Depending on your style of air fryer, either add all the vegetables directly to the drawer or use a silicone liner.

Add the pesto, basil and garlic granules and season to taste. Spray with low-calorie cooking spray and mix well.

Air-fry at 190°C for 20 minutes, stirring halfway through.

Add the feta and cook for a further 5–10 minutes. The vegetables should be soft and browning around the edges.

Meanwhile, cook the pasta according to the packet instructions (we cooked ours for 10 minutes), then drain well.

Add the roasted vegetables to a food processor and blitz until smooth, adding a little splash of water to loosen the sauce, if needed.

Add the cooked pasta back to the air fryer, pour over the sauce and stir to coat. Sprinkle over the cheese and cook for a further 5 minutes until golden and bubbly.

TIP:
Use any tomatoes you like, we used a combination of yellow and red cherry tomatoes and some large tomatoes, too.

DAIRY FREE

GLUTEN FREE
USE GF SOY SAUCE AND MISO PASTE

LOW CARB

HIGH PROTEIN

SESAME and GINGER COD

⏱ **5 MINS + 30 MINS MARINATING (OPTIONAL)**   **10 MINS**   ✕ **SERVES 2**

PER SERVING:
187 KCAL / 6.8G CARBS

2 tsp miso paste
1 garlic clove, peeled and crushed
small piece of root ginger, peeled and grated
2 tsp sesame oil
1 tsp runny honey
2 x 120g chunky cod loins
1 tsp toasted sesame seeds
1 pak choi, sliced in half lengthways
1 tbsp soy sauce

TO ACCOMPANY:
125g cooked basmati rice
 (+ 173 kcal per serving)

You'll be amazed what a quick marinade can do in this speedy midweek dinner! These cod loins are coated in a salty, garlicky miso and ginger paste – with a drizzle of sesame oil that brings a toasty depth of flavour. They're cooked to perfection in the air fryer alongside pak choi, which turns tender and caramelized in minutes. Light, fragrant and full of umami goodness… fish night just got upgraded!

In a bowl, mix the miso, garlic, ginger, 1 teaspoon of the sesame oil and honey together until well combined.

Pat the cod loins dry with a paper towel, then smother them in the paste. Cover and allow to marinate for 30 minutes. This is optional, but will improve the flavour.

Sprinkle the top of the cod with the sesame seeds.

Line the air fryer basket with a piece of non-stick baking paper and add the cod to the basket.

Rub the remaining teaspoon of sesame oil into the pak choi halves and add them to the air fryer. Sprinkle the soy sauce over the pak choi.

Air-fry for 8–10 minutes, depending on the thickness of your cod. When cooked, the cod should be opaque and the pak choi will be tender in the centre and charred and crisp on the edges.

TIPS:
Slice the pak choi lengthways through the root to keep the leaves together.

If you haven't got them ready-toasted, you can toast your own sesame seeds in a dry frying pan over a high heat for a minute or two until golden. Keep them moving and be careful not to let them catch, as they can become bitter.

BAKES and ROASTS

BAKES and ROASTS

SWEET CHILLI HALLOUMI-STUFFED CHICKEN

🕐 **15 MINS**   🍲 **25–30 MINS**   ✖ **SERVES 4**

PER SERVING:
326 KCAL /11G CARBS

2 tsp garlic granules
2 tsp onion granules
1 tsp dried oregano
½ tsp chilli flakes
4 chicken breasts, approx. 125g each
225g reduced-fat halloumi
salt and freshly ground black pepper, to taste

FOR THE SWEET CHILLI COATING:
2 tsp chilli flakes
1 tbsp honey
4 tsp sriracha
2 tsp rice vinegar
1 tbsp granulated sweetener

TO ACCOMPANY:
75g mixed salad (+ 15 kcal per serving)

Give your chicken breasts a glow up with this sweet and salty twist on your usual chicken dinner! We've sliced the chicken, hasselback-style, to create pockets perfect for stuffing with thick slices of halloumi cheese. Smother in a tangy, sweet and spicy chilli sauce and pop in the air fryer until it's cooked to crispy, juicy perfection. Serve simply with a fresh salad for a high-protein, high-flavour sensation.

In a small bowl, combine the garlic granules, onion granules, oregano and chilli flakes and season to taste with salt and pepper.

Using a sharp knife, make four cuts across each chicken breast, slicing almost to the bottom but not through it. Sprinkle over the herb mixture and rub all over the surface of the chicken breasts.

Cut the halloumi into eight slices, then cut each slice in half again. Place a slice of halloumi into each cut in the chicken breasts.

Line the air fryer with non-stick baking paper and place the chicken breasts into the basket. You may need to cook in batches depending on the size of your air fryer. Air-fry at 180°C for 10 minutes.

In a small bowl, combine all the sweet chilli coating ingredients.

Brush the chicken breasts with half of the sweet chilli coating and cook for a further 15–20 minutes, basting a few more times throughout the cooking, until the chicken is cooked through and no pinkness remains.

Serve with your choice of accompaniment.

PESTO CHICKEN TRAYBAKE

⏱ **15 MINS**   🍲 **40 MINS**   ✕ **SERVES 4**

PER SERVING:
449 KCAL / 24G CARBS

500g new potatoes, sliced
4 tbsp reduced-fat green pesto
100g reduced-fat cream cheese
4 chicken breasts, approx. 130g each
8 smoked bacon medallions
low-calorie cooking spray
240g green beans, trimmed
160g asparagus, woody ends removed
100g cherry tomatoes, halved
salt and freshly ground black pepper, to taste

Did someone say chicken, bacon and pesto, all in one dish? You read that right – we've combined three classic favourite ingredients to create this mouthwatering traybake. It's chicken breast smothered in creamy green pesto, wrapped in rich and tasty bacon, and cooked off in the air fryer for a delicious caramelized finish. There's no need to add any sides either, making it the perfect midweek meal.

Add the potatoes to a pan of cold salted water. Bring to the boil and simmer for 5 minutes until just softened.

In a small bowl, combine the pesto and cream cheese and mix until smooth.

Using a sharp knife, make a pocket in the chicken breasts, cutting horizontally down the length of each breast, starting at the thickest part – be careful not to cut all the way through.

Fill these pockets with the cream cheese mixture and spread any remaining mixture on top. Secure with a cocktail stick and wrap the chicken breasts in the bacon medallions.

Depending on the style of your air fryer, either place the chicken pieces and potatoes into a silicone liner or line the basket with non-stick baking paper. Spray with low-calorie cooking spray. Air-fry at 180°C for 20 minutes.

Add the green beans, asparagus and tomatoes. Respray and season to taste with salt and pepper. Continue to cook for a further 15 minutes until the chicken is cooked through and no sign of pinkness remains.

Divide the chicken, potatoes, green beans, asparagus and tomatoes between the plates and serve.

LIGHT BITES

VEGGIE

 VEGAN
USE DF YOGHURT

 FREEZE ME

BATCH COOK

DAIRY FREE
USE DF YOGHURT

GLUTEN FREE

EASY TO HALVE
SEE INDEX

INDIAN-STYLE SWEET POTATO FRIES *and* RAITA

🕐 **10 MINS**   📦 **20 MINS**   ✕ **SERVES 4**

PER SERVING:
173 KCAL /33G CARBS

FOR THE SWEET POTATO FRIES:
4 medium sweet potatoes, peeled and cut into 1.5cm (⅝in) thick fries, approx. 600g
low-calorie cooking spray
1 tbsp mild curry powder
1 tsp garlic granules
salt and freshly ground black pepper, to taste

FOR THE RAITA:
100g cucumber, deseeded and coarsely grated
150g fat-free Greek yoghurt
10 fresh mint leaves (stalks removed), finely chopped
1 tsp white granulated sweetener
¼ tsp garlic granules

You only need a couple of spices to make these fries – and they're a taste sensation. We've tossed them in a simple blend of curry powder and garlic, giving them a delicious Indian-inspired flavour that perfectly complements the natural sweetness of the potato. And there's no deep-fat fryer in sight – your air fryer keeps the calories down and cooks your fries in just 20 minutes! Spice things up even more with medium or even hot curry powder, and serve with our refreshing mint raita on the side.

Place the sweet potato fries in a large bowl and spray with low-calorie cooking spray. Sprinkle over the curry powder and garlic granules and toss to coat evenly.

Place the fries into the air fryer basket. Depending on the size of your air fryer, you may need to cook the fries in batches. Air-fry at 160°C for 20 minutes, or until the fries are soft inside and some are starting to brown a little around the edges. Season well with salt and pepper. If any of the curry and garlic seasoning is left in the air fryer, sprinkle it over the fries before serving.

While the fries are cooking, make the raita. Place the grated cucumber in a clean kitchen towel and squeeze out as much liquid as possible. Discard the liquid and put the cucumber in a small bowl.

Add the yoghurt, mint, sweetener, garlic granules and mix to combine. Season to taste with salt and pepper. Place in the fridge until ready to serve.

Serve the fries alongside the dip.

TIP:
Freeze the prepared raw sweet potato fries before adding the seasoning. Season, then air-fry from frozen for about 20–25 minutes, or until soft inside and starting to brown around the edges.

USE DF MAYONNAISE

USE GF BREADCRUMBS

COCONUT SALMON BITES

 10 MINS    8 MINS   ✕ SERVES 2

PER SERVING:
343 KCAL / 7.6G CARBS

10g panko breadcrumbs
10g desiccated coconut
¼ tsp smoked sweet paprika
2 x 110g skinless salmon fillets, each cut into 8 cubes
low-calorie cooking spray
1 tbsp lighter-than-light mayonnaise
1 tbsp light sweet chilli sauce
1 tbsp lime juice
salt and freshly ground black pepper, to taste
a few coriander leaves, to garnish
lime wedges, to serve

TO ACCOMPANY:
75g mixed salad (+ 15 kcal per serving) and small sweet potato, baked (+ 124 kcal per serving)

Looking for a flavour-packed light dinner that's ready in under 20 minutes? We've got you covered. Crafting these salmon bites is as simple as rolling chunks of salmon in coconut and panko breadcrumbs, then letting your air fryer take over. In the meantime, mix mayo, sweet chilli sauce and lime juice to make a tangy dip. If you fancy something on the side, why not try baked sweet potato or an Asian-inspired salad? The ideal midweek meal!

Mix the breadcrumbs, coconut, smoked paprika and some salt and pepper together in a small bowl.

Add the salmon cubes and toss around until well coated. Lightly press the crumbs into the salmon.

Spray the air fryer basket with low-calorie cooking spray. Add the coated cubes of salmon, leaving a gap between each to allow even cooking. Air-fry at 200°C for 8 minutes, shaking the basket halfway through.

While the salmon cooks, mix the mayonnaise, sweet chilli sauce and lime juice together in a small bowl, to make your dip.

When the salmon is cooked it should be golden on the outside and opaque but still moist inside.

Serve garnished with a few coriander leaves, with the dipping sauce and extra lime wedges for squeezing!

TIPS:

If you like spice, swap the smoked paprika for chilli powder.

This is best served fresh, as freezing and reheating can dry out the delicate salmon, however leftovers can be frozen using standard guidelines (see page 15).

BRIE and HONEY DOUGH BALLS

🕐 20 MINS + 1½ HOURS RESTING   🗑 10–12 MINS   ✕ MAKES 16

PER SERVING:
87 KCAL /13G CARBS

250g strong white flour, plus extra for dusting
2 tsp fast-action dried yeast
½ tsp caster sugar
½ tsp salt
150ml warm water
100g brie, rind removed and cut into 16 even pieces
2 tbsp runny honey
¼–½ tsp chilli flakes, depending on how spicy you want them

TIPS:
If you don't like chilli heat, leave out the flakes. It'll still be delicious. Or for extra heat, sprinkle over a few more!

Although these are best served fresh, they can be frozen before coating with the honey. Once defrosted, warm through for a few minutes in the air fryer or oven and brush with the honey as per recipe.

These Brie and Honey Dough Balls are pure indulgence, for only 87 calories each! We're talking fluffy, golden dough balls stuffed with creamy, melted Brie and brushed with a gorgeous chilli honey glaze. Air-fry in just 12 minutes, once ready they're ridiculously puffed and irresistible. Not a fan of heat? No worries, reduce or ditch the chilli flakes completely. We love these served alongside our comforting Roasted Vegetable Pasta Bake (page 134).

Sift the flour into a large mixing bowl. Add the yeast, caster sugar and salt and stir well.

Make a well in the centre and add the warm water, then mix until it comes together in a ball.

Tip out onto a lightly floured surface and start to knead the dough, using the heel of your hand to stretch and fold the dough. Knead for about 10 minutes until the dough is smooth and elastic.

Shape into a ball and return to the mixing bowl. Cover with cling film and leave in a warm place for around 1 hour, until doubled in size.

Knock back the dough and knead four or five times. Divide into 16 even pieces. Run the air fryer for 30 seconds to warm it up, but do not allow it to become too hot, then turn it off.

Roll each portion of dough into a ball and flatten out. Place a piece of brie in the centre and fold the edges around to enclose the brie. Pinch the edges together to seal.

Line the air fryer drawer with a liner or piece of non-stick baking paper. Place the stuffed dough balls, sealed-side down, in the lined drawer, leaving a 1cm (½in) gap between each. Leave in the warm air fryer to prove for 30 minutes. The dough balls should increase in size and become puffy.

Air-fry the proved dough balls at 180°C for 10–12 minutes, shaking the drawer or flipping the dough balls halfway through.

While the dough balls cook, place the honey and chilli flakes in a small bowl and microwave for 15 seconds. Alternatively, you

can melt in a small pan on the stove. This will make the honey runnier and easier to brush over the cooked dough balls.

When the dough balls are cooked and golden and still hot, use a pastry brush to coat the tops and sides with the chilli honey. Allow to cool slightly before removing from the air fryer and serving.

FREEZE WITHOUT SWEET CHILLI SAUCE

USE GF PASTRY

CHILLI CHEESE SLICES

⏱ **15 MINS** 🗑 **12 MINS** ✕ **MAKES 8**

PER SERVING:
228 KCAL /20G CARBS

120g Gouda, finely grated
3 spring onions, finely chopped
½ red chilli, deseeded and finely diced
8g fresh coriander leaves (stalks removed), roughly chopped
1 medium egg, beaten
320g ready-rolled light puff pastry sheet
1 tsp skimmed milk
4 tsp reduced-sugar Thai sweet chilli sauce
salt and freshly ground black pepper, to taste

TO ACCOMPANY:
75g mixed salad (+ 15 kcal per serving)

These tasty Chilli Cheese Slices are proper comfort food with a punchy twist. Picture this: gloriously golden puff pastry topped with melted cheese, fresh coriander and just the right amount of chilli heat. Ready in just 12 minutes, these beauties are perfect for popping in your lunchbox or serving with a crisp salad. We've used ready-rolled light puff pastry and reduced-sugar Thai sweet chilli sauce to keep things easy and slimming friendly, without compromising on those irresistible flavours!

Place the cheese, spring onions, red chilli, coriander and beaten egg in a medium bowl and season well with salt and pepper. Mix together to form a stiff paste and set aside.

Unroll the pastry sheet, leaving it on the paper backing and place it on a work surface. Cut into eight rectangles, each 9 x 12cm (3½ x 5in). Use a sharp knife to score a border around each pastry rectangle, 1cm (½in) in from the edge, taking care not to cut right through.

Divide the cheese mixture between the pastry rectangles, leaving the borders around the edges clear. Push down a little and spread out to cover the middle sections.

Brush the borders with a little milk. Line the air fryer drawer with non-stick baking paper and place the pastry slices onto the paper. You may need to cook these in batches depending on the size of your air fryer.

Air-fry at 170°C for 8 minutes, then flip the slices and cook for a further 4 minutes.

Remove from the air fryer and brush the cheese filling with sweet chilli sauce before serving.

TIP:
You could swap Gouda for Cheddar, if you prefer, and adjust the calories accordingly.

LIGHT BITES

153

VEGGIE
SWAP HAM FOR A VEGGIE OPTION

VEGAN
SWAP HAM FOR A VEGAN OPTION, USE VEGAN MOZZARELLA ALTERNATIVE

DAIRY FREE
USE DF CHEESE ALTERNATIVE

GLUTEN FREE
USE GF CRUMPETS

HIGH PROTEIN

EASY TO HALVE
SEE INDEX

PIZZA CRUMPETS

 **10 MINS**  **6 MINS** ✗ **MAKES 4**

PER SERVING:
179 KCAL /21G CARBS

4 crumpets
4 slices of wafer-thin ham, diced
2 sun-dried tomatoes, finely diced
100g reduced-fat mozzarella
freshly ground black pepper, to taste

FOR THE SAUCE:
2 tbsp tomato puree
1 tbsp water
¼ tsp garlic granules
½ tsp dried Italian mixed herbs
¼ tsp granulated sweetener (or sugar)

With enough imagination and an air fryer, anything can be a pizza. An easy-to-assemble light bite, these can be whipped up in just 15 minutes for a hasty, tasty lunch. With a sauce that can be made with a few store-cupboard essentials, this recipe doesn't even require a trip to the shops. For toppings, we've used ham and sun-dried tomatoes, but you can substitute for whatever's in your fridge – and Cheddar works just as well as mozzarella for a deliciously melty finish. We can't wait to see what you come up with!

Put all the sauce ingredients into a small bowl and stir until well combined.

Spread the sauce evenly over the tops of the crumpets, and top with the ham and sun-dried tomatoes.

Tear the mozzarella into pieces and divide between the crumpets. Season the crumpets with black pepper.

Place the pizza crumpets into the basket of the air fryer and air-fry at 180°C for 6 minutes until the bottom of the crumpets are crisp and the cheese is bubbling and golden. Serve!

PERI-PERI CHICKEN NUGGETS

 10 MINS + MARINATING OVERNIGHT    20 MINS   ✕ SERVES 4

PER SERVING:
206 KCAL / 13G CARBS

100g fat-free Greek yoghurt
2 tsp dried oregano
2 tsp garlic granules
2 tsp onion granules
1 tsp smoked paprika
1 tsp chilli flakes
½ tsp ground ginger
320g chicken breast, chopped into 3–4cm (1¼–1½in) pieces
70g panko breadcrumbs
2 tsp peri-peri seasoning
½ tsp garlic granules
low-calorie cooking spray
salt and freshly ground black pepper, to taste

FOR THE DIP:
40g fat-free Greek yoghurt
2 tbsp reduced-fat mayonnaise
juice of 1 lime

TO ACCOMPANY:
75g mixed salad (+ 15 kcal per serving)

Got a craving for your favourite deep-fried snack? We've got just the thing. These Peri-Peri Chicken Nuggets taste exactly the same as the ones you'll find in the takeaway or freezer aisle – only they're not coated in oil. Cook them in just 20 minutes in your air fryer – but don't forget to marinate them overnight. Trust us when we say it's a game-changer!

In a non-reactive bowl, combine the yoghurt, oregano, garlic granules, onion granules, paprika, chilli flakes and ginger, mix until smooth and season to taste with salt and pepper.

Add the chicken chunks and mix until fully coated, then cover and pop into the fridge overnight to marinate.

The next day, add the breadcrumbs to a bowl with the peri-peri seasoning and garlic granules. Dip each chicken piece into the breadcrumb mixture to completely coat on all sides.

Place the coated chicken pieces into the air fryer basket and spray with low-calorie cooking spray. You may need to cook in batches, depending on the size of your air fryer.

Air-fry at 170°C for 15–20 minutes until the nuggets are crispy and golden. To test that the chicken is cooked, cut a piece in half, the juices should run clear and there should be no pink remaining.

While the nuggets cook, make the dip. Add the yoghurt, mayonnaise and lime juice to a small bowl, mix until smooth and season to taste with salt and pepper.

Serve the nuggets with the dip alongside.

FRUIT and VEGETABLE CRISPS and DIPS – *Vegetables*

15 MINS **40 MINS** **SERVES 4**

PER SERVING:
136 KCAL /19G CARBS

SPECIAL EQUIPMENT:
Mandoline or sharp knife, high-speed blender or food processor

250g carrots (no need to peel)
250g parsnips (no need to peel)
low-calorie cooking spray
200g fat-free cottage cheese
25g sun-dried tomatoes, drained
1 tsp sun-dried tomato paste
8 basil leaves
2 tbsp milk (use whichever you have in your fridge)
salt and freshly ground black pepper, to taste

Crisps and dips are the ultimate snack – and you can double-dip to your heart's content with these low-fat alternatives to standard tortilla chips. We've thinly sliced carrots and parsnips and baked them in the air fryer to give them that satisfying crunch – with a tangy sun-dried tomato dip on the side.

Scrub the carrots and parsnips clean and pat dry with some paper towel. Carefully use a mandoline or sharp knife to cut them into thin, 3mm (⅛in) slices. There is no need to peel them first – the skin is the most nutritious part – but you can if you want.

Place in a bowl and spray well with low-calorie cooking spray. Season with a good pinch of salt.

Add a layer of carrots and parsnips to the air fryer basket. It is okay if they overlap a little, but do try to keep it to an even single layer. You will need to cook in two batches. Air-fry at 150°C for 20 minutes, shaking the basket occasionally, to ensure even cooking.

While the crisps cook, place the cottage cheese, sun-dried tomatoes, tomato paste, basil and milk in a high-speed blender. Blitz until smooth and velvety. Season with some salt and pepper.

When the carrots and parsnips are crisp and golden, empty out onto a plate lined with a piece of paper towel, and allow to cool while you cook the second batch.

When the crisps have cooled, arrange around the bowl of tomato and basil dip, and serve!

FRUIT and VEGETABLE CRISPS and DIPS – *Fruit*

🕒 **15 MINS** 🍳 **40 MINS** ✕ **SERVES 4**

PER SERVING:
120 KCAL / 19G CARBS

SPECIAL EQUIPMENT:
Mandoline or sharp knife, high-speed blender or food processor

2 crisp eating apples, cored
2 firm pears (slightly under-ripe are best)
low-calorie cooking spray
75g reduced-fat cream cheese
75g fat-free Greek yoghurt
1 tbsp maple syrup
1 tsp ground cinnamon
1 tsp granulated sweetener (optional)

If you've got a sweet tooth, cook slivers of apples and pears just the same way, and indulge in our velvety cinnamon dip. It's low in sugar and tastes like cheesecake… a win-win!

Slice the cored apples and the pears into thin slices, about 3mm (⅛in) thick. There is no need to core the pears first, but you may need to remove a few seeds from the larger slices. A mandoline is ideal for this, but do make sure to use it safely. Alternatively, a small sharp knife and a little care will do a good job.

Spray the air fryer basket with low-calorie cooking spray and add a layer of fruit slices. It is okay if they overlap a little, but try to keep it to an even, single layer. You will have to cook these in two batches.

Air-fry at 150°C for about 20 minutes, giving the basket a shake every 5 minutes or so, until the fruit is browned and crisp.

Empty the crisps onto a plate lined with a paper towel and leave to cool down and dry out while you cook the second batch of crisps.

While the second batch cooks, put the cream cheese, yoghurt, maple syrup and cinnamon in a bowl and beat until smooth. Add some granulated sweetener, to taste, if you wish.

Serve the cooled crisps with the cheesecake dip on the side.

TIPS:
Use firm, under-ripe pears for the best results.

The crisps keep for 3–4 days in an airtight container, but will become softer and slightly chewy as the days go by. They will still be a delicious snack.

BUFFALO CHICKEN SANDWICH

🕐 **15 MINS**   🍳 **25 MINS**   ✕ **SERVES 4**

PER SERVING:
419 KCAL / 43G CARBS

SPECIAL EQUIPMENT:
Food processor or stick blender

300g chicken breast, chopped into 5cm (2in) chunks
1 tsp garlic granules
1 tsp onion granules
1 tsp paprika
1 tbsp buffalo hot sauce
60g reduced-fat cream cheese
30g Stilton
1 tsp honey
50g red cabbage, finely shredded
1 medium carrot, peeled and cut into matchsticks
40g gherkins, sliced into strips
1 celery stick, diced
2 tbsp pickling vinegar, from the jar of gherkins
100g fat-free Greek yoghurt
salt and freshly ground black pepper, to taste
4 brioche rolls, sliced in half, to serve

Nothing beats a good old sandwich... especially when it's as tasty as this one. We've coated chicken in a tasty blend of garlic, onion and paprika, and air-fried it to perfection. Shredded into juicy pieces, tossed in spicy buffalo sauce, stuffed into deliciously soft brioche buns and topped with a pickled creamy slaw, it's a crispy, juicy crowd pleaser. We challenge you to taste it and not love it! Serve it on its own for a light lunch, or make it a meal with a side of fries.

Add the chicken to a bowl and sprinkle over the garlic granules, onion granules and paprika. Toss to coat.

Depending on the style of your air fryer, either place the chicken pieces into the drawer (after removing the basket) or place them into a silicone mould. Air-fry at 180°C for 15 minutes, turning halfway through.

Place the hot sauce, cream cheese, Stilton, honey and a splash of water into a small food processor or use a stick blender to blitz until a smooth, creamy consistency is achieved. Add a little more water, if needed.

Pour the sauce over the chicken and air-fry for another 10 minutes. The chicken should be cooked through with no pink remaining.

In a large bowl, combine the cabbage, carrot, gherkins, celery, pickling vinegar and yoghurt. Mix well to coat and season to taste with salt and pepper.

Transfer the chicken and sauce from the air fryer into a bowl and shred the chicken pieces using two forks. Stir well so the sauce coats the shredded chicken.

Build the sandwiches in the rolls with the pulled chicken and slaw on top.

USE PLANT-BASED YOGHURT AND MAYO

USE DF YOGHURT AND MAYO

SEE INDEX

CRISPY CHILLI POTATO SALAD

🕙 **10 MINS**   🍲 **30 MINS**   ✕ **SERVES 4**

PER SERVING:
181 KCAL / 30G CARBS

500g new potatoes, sliced in half
low-calorie cooking spray
100g fat-free Greek yoghurt
1 tbsp rice vinegar
2 tbsp honey
1 tbsp sriracha
½ tbsp garlic granules
½ tbsp chilli flakes
2 tbsp reduced-fat mayonnaise
1 red chilli, deseeded and finely sliced
6g chives, finely chopped
salt and freshly ground black pepper, to taste

This recipe is perfect for barbecues and summer spreads! We've lightly crushed baby potatoes and air-fried them until the edges are crisp, then tossed them in a sweet chilli dressing made with honey, sriracha and creamy Greek yoghurt. It's got just the right balance of heat, sweetness and crunch. Perfect for weeknight dinners or anywhere your usual spuds need a glow-up.

Add the potatoes to a pan of cold salted water. Bring to the boil, then reduce the heat and simmer for 8 minutes until just tender.

Add the potatoes directly to the drawer of the air fryer. Squash flat with the bottom of a glass. Spray with low-calorie cooking spray and season to taste with salt and pepper.

Air-fry at 200°C for 20 minutes until crispy and golden brown.

In a large bowl, combine the yoghurt, rice vinegar, honey, sriracha, garlic, chili flakes and mayonnaise and mix until smooth. Leave to one side.

Once the potatoes are cooked, add them to the yoghurt mixture and stir to coat. Alternatively, spread the yoghurt mixture over a serving platter and top with the crispy potatoes. Sprinkle over the sliced chilli and chives and serve.

TIP:
The potatoes will lose some of their crispness once the dressing is added, so will go soggy if prepared too far in advance.

CAJUN-STYLE STEAK SALAD

⏱ **15 MINS**   🍲 **10 MINS**   ✕ **SERVES 2**

PER SERVING:
428 KCAL / 24G CARBS

FOR THE SPICE MIX:
2 tsp paprika
2 tsp ground coriander
2 tsp ground cumin
1 tsp dried oregano
½–1 tsp chilli powder, to taste

FOR THE DRESSING:
75g fat-free Greek yoghurt
30g blue Stilton, crumbled
juice of ½ lime
1–2 tbsp water
salt and freshly ground black pepper, to taste

FOR THE CROUTONS:
1 medium slice sourdough bread (or your preferred bread)
low-calorie cooking spray
1 tsp garlic granules

FOR THE SALAD:
400g thick-cut rump steak, fat removed, cut into 2cm (¾in) cubes (approx. 320g when trimmed)
low-calorie cooking spray
2 handfuls of mixed salad leaves
10 cherry tomatoes, halved
½ small red onion, peeled and sliced
½ green pepper, deseeded and sliced
75g tinned sweetcorn, drained
handful of fresh coriander leaves, roughly chopped, to garnish

Looking for a steak salad with a bit of punch? This one's got it all! Juicy chunks of Cajun-spiced steak, crunchy golden croutons and a zingy blue cheese dressing, all served over a rainbow of fresh salad veg. It's quick to whip up in the air fryer and full of bold, satisfying flavours. Whether you're cooking for a midweek treat or a light weekend lunch, this one's a proper showstopper.

Mix all the herbs and spices together for the Cajun spice mix. This will make enough for three to four salads, so store in an airtight jar.

Next, make the dressing. Place the yoghurt, Stilton and lime juice in a small bowl and mash together with a fork. Add a tablespoon or two of water to reach a creamy, coating consistency. Season with salt and pepper to taste. Cover and store in the fridge until needed.

Now prepare the croutons. Tear the bread into rough chunks, place in a bowl and spray liberally with low-calorie cooking spray. Sprinkle over the garlic granules, season with salt and pepper and toss around until the bread is well coated. Air-fry for 5 minutes at 180°C until crisp and golden. Set aside.

Spray the steak with low-calorie cooking spray and use 2 teaspoons of the Cajun spice mix to coat the chunks. Preheat the air fryer to 200°C. If your air fryer doesn't have a preheat function, run it for 3 minutes at 200°C.

When the air fryer is hot, add the steak chunks and air-fry for 2–5 minutes, depending on how you like your steak (2 minutes should be medium/rare and 5 minutes well done).

Assemble the salad ingredients on plates, top with the steak and croutons and drizzle with the blue cheese dressing. Sprinkle the chopped coriander on top and serve.

TIP:
Timings are for steak cooked straight from the fridge. If your steak has come to room temperature, you will need to cook for less time.

LIGHT BITES

SPROUT and TAHINI SALAD

🕐 10 MINS 🍲 15 MINS ✕ SERVES 2

PER SERVING:
273 KCAL / 9.1G CARBS

200g sprouts, cut in half
200g broccoli, cut into bite-size pieces
low-calorie cooking spray
1 tsp garlic granules
½ tsp dried thyme
2 tbsp tahini
juice of 1 lemon
1 tbsp cold water
salt and freshly ground black pepper, to taste
15g pecans, chopped

Who said sprouts are just for Christmas? This fresh, zesty salad makes them the star of the show, pairing air-fried Brussels with tender broccoli and a tasty lemon-tahini dressing. Finished with a sprinkle of chopped pecans for crunch, it's a speedy, plant-based side that'll brighten up your plate. Whether you're serving it as a side with grilled chicken, a traybake or a veggie main, it's a keeper all year round.

Add the sprouts and broccoli to the air fryer basket and spray with low-calorie cooking spray. Sprinkle over the garlic and thyme and toss to coat.

Cook at 180°C for 12–15 minutes until the vegetables are soft and turning crispy around the edges.

In a small bowl, combine the tahini and lemon juice and mix. Add the water a teaspoon at a time until the dressing is smooth. You may not need all the water. Season to taste with salt and pepper.

Drizzle the dressing over the vegetables and sprinkle over the chopped pecans. Serve.

ASPARAGUS, BROCCOLI and FETA SALAD

🕐 **10 MINS**   🍲 **10 MINS**   ✗ **SERVES 2**

PER SERVING:
270 KCAL / 9G CARBS

SPECIAL EQUIPMENT:
Food processor or mini chopper

360g asparagus, each spear broken in half
320g Tenderstem broccoli
low-calorie cooking spray
1 tsp garlic granules
100g reduced-fat feta cheese
40g fat-free Greek yoghurt
juice of ½ lemon
100g edamame beans
1 spring onion, finely sliced
salt and freshly ground black pepper, to taste

Salads just got even simpler, thanks to your air fryer. Packed with springtime greens and topped with tangy feta cheese, this super-light salad is ready in just 20 minutes – talk about the perfect midweek meal. Prepping is as simple as chopping your veg, and then you can hand the rest of the hard work over to your favourite gadget. When the weather warms up and the sun is shining, invite your best friend to share this perfect al fresco lunch!

Add the asparagus and broccoli to the air fryer basket and spray with low-calorie cooking spray.

Sprinkle over the garlic granules and season to taste with salt and pepper. Crumble over 70g of the feta.

Cook at 180°C for 8–10 minutes until the asparagus and broccoli are softening and just turning brown on the edges.

While the vegetables cook, add the remaining feta, yoghurt and lemon juice to a mini chopper or food processor and blitz until smooth. Season to taste with salt and pepper. Set aside.

Add the edamame beans to a small pan and cover with boiling water. Bring to the boil, then reduce the heat and cook for 2 minutes. Drain.

Once cooked, add the broccoli, asparagus and feta to serving plates. Add the edamame beans and sliced spring onion and drizzle over the dressing. Serve.

TIP:
Alternatively, you can cook the vegetables and feta in an oven at 200°C for 12–15 minutes.

VEGGIE

 VEGAN
USE VEGAN-STYLE FETA CHEESE AND DF YOGHURT

 BATCH COOK

 DAIRY FREE
USE VEGAN-STYLE FETA CHEESE AND DF YOGHURT

 HIGH PROTEIN

 EASY TO HALVE
SEE INDEX

SPICED CAULIFLOWER and CRANBERRY COUSCOUS

🕒 15 MINS   🍲 16 MINS   ✕ SERVES 4

PER SERVING:
193 KCAL / 28G CARBS

- 250g cauliflower, cut into bite-size pieces
- low-calorie cooking spray
- 2 tsp garlic granules
- 1 tsp ground coriander
- 1 tsp ground cumin
- 1 tsp smoked paprika
- ½ tsp ground turmeric
- 1 x 400g tin chickpeas, drained and rinsed
- 100g giant couscous
- 70g fat-free Greek yoghurt
- juice of ½ lemon
- 2 tsp honey
- ½ tsp sriracha
- 40g reduced-fat feta cheese, crumbled
- 20g dried cranberries
- salt and freshly ground black pepper, to taste

Discover just how versatile cauliflower can be with this fruity cauliflower couscous. Totalling under 200 calories, it's light and nourishing – filled with protein-packed chickpeas and light and nutty couscous that keeps you fuller for longer. We've perfected an aromatic spice mix to give things a little kick, and it also adds a warmth to the recipe. Perfect for summer barbecues or transitioning into the cooler season!

Add the cauliflower to a bowl and spray well with low-calorie cooking spray. Sprinkle over the garlic, coriander, cumin, paprika and turmeric and season to taste with salt and pepper. Toss to coat.

Add the cauliflower to the air fryer basket and cook at 180°C for 8 minutes.

Add the chickpeas and mix to incorporate. Cook for a further 8 minutes.

While the cauliflower and chickpeas are cooking, add the couscous to a pan of boiling water and cook according to the packet instructions (we cooked ours for 10 minutes), then drain well.

In a small bowl, combine the yoghurt, lemon juice, honey and sriracha. Mix well and season to taste.

Add the roasted cauliflower, chickpeas and couscous to a large serving bowl and mix well. Sprinkle over the feta and cranberries, then drizzle over the dressing and serve.

TIP:
Alternatively, you can cook the vegetables and feta in an oven at 200°C for 12–15 minutes.

VEGGIE
USE VEGETARIAN ITALIAN HARD CHEESE

VEGAN
USE VEGAN PARMESAN ALTERNATIVE

FREEZE ME
SOUP ONLY

BATCH COOK

DAIRY FREE
USE VEGAN PARMESAN ALTERNATIVE

GLUTEN FREE
USE GF STOCK AND BREAD ROLL

EASY TO HALVE
SEE INDEX

ROASTED TOMATO and GARLIC SOUP

🕐 10 MINS   🍲 31–36 MINS   ✕ SERVES 4

Air fryers aren't just for chips, they're brilliant for roasting fresh veggies too! This recipe transforms a bowlful of salad tomatoes into a rich, flavour-packed soup that's as simple as it is satisfying. We've air-fried the garlic and tomatoes to enhance their natural sweetness, then blitzed them with fresh basil and balsamic vinegar for a light lunch that tastes like it's simmered for hours. Serve with our garlicky, Parmesan croutons for a little extra crunch.

PER SERVING:
121 KCAL /15G CARBS

SPECIAL EQUIPMENT:
Food processor

FOR THE CROUTONS:
60g wholemeal bread roll
low-calorie cooking spray
½ tsp garlic granules
15g Parmesan, finely grated
salt and freshly ground black pepper, to taste

FOR THE SOUP:
12 salad tomatoes, around 850g in total
6 garlic cloves, peeled
low-calorie cooking spray
400ml vegetable stock (1 vegetable stock cube dissolved in 400ml boiling water)
1 tbsp tomato puree
1 tsp balsamic vinegar
a handful of fresh basil leaves

TO ACCOMPANY *(optional)*:
60g wholemeal bread roll (+ 146 kcal per serving)

First, make the croutons. Tear the bread roll into rustic pieces and place in a bowl. Spray well with low-calorie cooking spray. Sprinkle over the garlic granules and Parmesan, season with salt and pepper and toss to coat the bread evenly.

Air-fry at 170°C for 6 minutes, shaking the drawer halfway through.

While the croutons cook, prepare the tomatoes by cutting in half, from top to bottom. Use a small knife to remove the stalk by cutting a small v out of the top of each half.

When the croutons are cooked – they should be crisp and golden – place on a plate and leave to cool.

Wipe out your air fryer and add the tomato halves, keeping the cut sides facing upwards as much as possible. You can squeeze them in and overlap slightly, if you need to. Add the garlic cloves, spray well with low-calorie cooking spray and season with salt and pepper.

Air-fry at 180°C for 25–30 minutes. The tomatoes should be lightly charred around the edges.

Place the tomatoes and garlic in a food processor along with the hot stock, tomato puree, balsamic vinegar and basil. Blitz until it reaches your desired consistency. Season with salt and pepper to taste and serve immediately, sprinkled with the Parmesan croutons.

TIP:
Calories in soup only – 64.
Calories in croutons – 57.

SWEET TREATS

USE GF PASTRY

APRICOT TARTE TATIN

⏱ 15 MINS + 30 MINS COOLING   🍲 25–30 MINS   ✕ SERVES 4

PER SERVING:
199 KCAL /26G CARBS

30g caster sugar
20g granulated sweetener
20ml cold water
20g butter
200g tinned apricot halves in natural juice
15 x 19cm (6 x 7½in) ready-rolled light puff pastry sheet, approx. 115g

TO ACCOMPANY *(optional)*:
60g low-calorie vanilla ice cream (+ 62 kcal per serving)

You won't believe something this delicious can be so simple to make! This Apricot Tarte Tatin is our slimming-friendly take on a French classic, made using a handful of easy ingredients. It all starts with a homemade caramel syrup, along with utterly fuss-free tinned apricots and ready-rolled buttery puff pastry. Once air-fried, you'll end up with a golden upside-down tart, ready to flip, slice and serve! It tastes absolutely divine with a scoop of low-calorie vanilla ice cream.

Add the sugar, sweetener and water to a small saucepan and set over a low heat. Heat for 8–10 minutes, stirring frequently until a pale golden colour. Add the butter and stir until fully combined.

Remove the basket from the air fryer and line the drawer with a sheet of non-stick baking paper. Alternatively, use a silicone mould or tin that fits inside your air fryer. Pour in the caramel syrup and arrange the apricots, cut-sides down, into the syrup.

Air-fry for 5 minutes at 180°C.

Place the sheet of puff pastry on top of the apricots, pressing down with your hands. Return to the air fryer for a further 10–15 minutes until the pastry is golden brown.

Leave to cool for 30 minutes. Using a fish slice to help you, lift the tart out of the air fryer, holding onto the non-stick baking paper.

Flip the tart over so that the puff pastry is now on the bottom. Slice and serve!

COOKIE DOUGH POTS

🕐 **5 MINS**   🗑 **10-12 MINS**   ✕ **SERVES 4**

PER SERVING:
254 KCAL /37G CARBS

SPECIAL EQUIPMENT:
**4 x 125ml ramekins,
7.8 x 4.5cm (3 x 2in)**

60g reduced-fat spread
30g caster sugar
30g granulated sweetener
1 medium egg
100g plain flour
2 tbsp cocoa powder
20g chocolate chips
  (we used a combination
  of dark and milk)

Remember the mug cake craze? Move over, microwave – your air fryer's got this one covered. These Cookie Dough Pots taste exactly like the gooey desserts from your favourite takeaway. And since they take just under 20 minutes to make, they're even faster than ordering in – not to mention healthier. Grab your mixing bowl to make the batter, give it some welly, and then let your favourite gadget work its magic. Once they're baked to perfection, you'll have a ready-to-serve dessert that melts in your mouth.

To a mixing bowl, add the spread, caster sugar and sweetener. Mix with a wooden spoon until creamy and combined.

Add the egg and mix again.

Add the flour and cocoa powder and mix again until smooth and fully combined. Add half of the chocolate chips and mix again.

Divide the mixture between the four ramekins and roughly smooth out the tops. Sprinkle the remaining chocolate on top.

Cook at 160°C for 10–12 minutes. You may need to do this in batches, depending on the size of your air fryer. The cookie pots should be crisp on top and still a little soft and gooey in the middle but not raw. Leave to stand for a minute and serve.

CASHEW MACAROONS

⏱ **10 MINS**   🍲 **17 MINS**   ✕ **SERVES 24**

PER SERVING:
51 KCAL /1.6G CARBS

SPECIAL EQUIPMENT:
High-speed blender or mini chopper

200g cashews
2 tbsp granulated sweetener
1 egg white, beaten
1 tsp vanilla extract
1 tsp icing sugar

Before you reach for the biscuits, try our Cashew Macaroons. These nutty little bites of goodness make a tasty on-the-go snack – and with just four ingredients and a little icing sugar for dusting, you can rustle them up in no time at all. No baking expertise required! Top tip – if you make a batch on Sunday, they'll keep all week. If they last that long, that is!

Reserve 24 cashew halves for decoration and add the rest to a high-speed blender or food processor. Blitz to a flour and place in a bowl with the granulated sweetener.

Beat the egg white with the vanilla extract and add to the cashew flour, bit by bit, mixing until it comes together in a soft, pliable dough.

Roll the dough into 24 evenly sized balls. Flatten them slightly and press a cashew half into the top of each.

Line the air fryer basket with non-stick baking paper or a silicone liner and add the macaroons. You will need to cook them in two batches.

Air-fry at 150°C for 12 minutes, then flip the macaroons and air-fry for a further 5 minutes to ensure you have a crisp bottom.

Remove from the air fryer and place on a cooling rack until cool. Dust with icing sugar and serve.

TIPS:
Will keep in an airtight container for up to a week.

Freeze in airtight bags. They will soften upon defrosting, but you can refresh them in the air fryer for a couple of minutes.

CHOCOLATE and BEETROOT MUFFINS

🕐 10 MINS   🍲 10 MINS   ✕ SERVES 12

VEGGIE

FREEZE ME

BATCH COOK

GLUTEN FREE
USE GF FLOUR AND BAKING POWDER

PER SERVING:
126 KCAL /17G CARBS

SPECIAL EQUIPMENT:
12 silicone or sturdy paper cupcake cases, blender or food processor

- 125g pre-cooked beetroot, cut into chunks
- 125g fat-free Greek yoghurt
- 2 medium eggs
- 50g reduced-fat spread
- 185g self-raising flour
- 15g cocoa powder
- 1 tsp baking powder
- 3 tbsp granulated sweetener (or sugar)
- 50g chocolate chips

Did you know that the 'red' in red velvet cakes originally came from beetroot? The brightly coloured cool-season crop makes the cake red and gives it a moist and fluffy texture. While our Chocolate and Beetroot Muffin batter might lose its pink hue once it's been in your air fryer, it does do the job of keeping our muffins light and airy. At just over 100 calories, they make for a delicious sweet treat or an indulgent addition to your breakfast.

Place the beetroot, yoghurt and eggs into a blender or food processor and blitz until smooth.

Melt the reduced-fat spread, either in the microwave or in a small pan.

Sift the flour, cocoa powder and baking powder into a mixing bowl and stir in the sweetener and chocolate chips.

Pour the melted spread and beetroot mix into the dry ingredients and use a spatula to stir until just combined. Try not to over-stir.

Divide the batter equally between the cupcake cases.

Place in the air fryer, leaving a little space for the air to circulate. Air-fry at 160°C for 10 minutes. You may need to do this in two batches.

To test whether they are cooked, insert a skewer into the centre. If it comes out clean, your muffins are cooked.

TIPS:

You can cook your own beetroot, but it is much easier to use pre-cooked beetroot, which can be bought in vacuum packs in the salad section of most supermarkets. Just make sure you don't pick up pickled beetroot by mistake!

Wrap individually and freeze in airtight containers.

SWEET TREATS

VEGGIE

FREEZE ME
CAKES ONLY

BATCH COOK

DAIRY FREE
USE DF SPREAD AND MILK

BISCOFF and BANANA CAKES

15 MINS + 30 MINS COOLING   15-20 MINS   SERVES 12

PER SERVING:
193 KCAL / 24G CARBS

SPECIAL EQUIPMENT:
Electric hand whisk
12 silicone or sturdy paper cupcake cases

180g reduced-fat spread
30g brown sugar
30g brown granulated sweetener
2 medium eggs
1 banana, peeled and mashed
180g self-raising flour
½ tsp baking powder
1 tbsp Biscoff spread
60g icing sugar
1 tbsp skimmed milk
1 Biscoff biscuit, crumbled

You'll need just one banana and a handful of simple ingredients to whip up some absolutely irresistible Biscoff and Banana Cakes. These moist, banana bread-style cupcakes are perfect for batch cooking and stashing away in the freezer. Once you're ready to serve, simply top with a swirl of creamy homemade Biscoff icing (plus a sprinkle of Biscoff biscuit for extra flavour and crunch!). They're the ultimate sweet pick-me-up with your afternoon cuppa.

To a mixing bowl, add the spread, sugar and sweetener. Beat using an electric hand whisk for 1 minute until creamy and combined.

Add the eggs and banana and whisk again. The mixture will look like it has curdled, but don't worry.

Add the flour and baking powder. Whisk for 1–2 minutes until the mixture has turned pale and is thick and creamy.

Divide the batter between 12 cupcake cases. Air-fry at 160°C for 15–20 minutes until a skewer inserted in the centre comes out clean. Leave to cool completely.

In a small bowl, combine the Biscoff spread, icing sugar and milk and mix until smooth.

Top each cake with a little of the icing and some of the crumbled biscuit.

SWEET TREATS

VEGGIE

VEGAN
USE DF YOGHURT AND SPREAD

DAIRY FREE
USE DF YOGHURT AND SPREAD

GLUTEN FREE
USE GF FLOUR AND BAKING POWDER

CINNAMON DOUGHNUT HOLES

⏱ **5 MINS**   🍲 **10 MINS**   ✖ **SERVES 4**

PER SERVING:
154 KCAL / 27G CARBS

120g plain flour
120g fat-free Greek yoghurt
½ tsp baking powder
1 tsp vanilla extract
low-calorie cooking spray
2 tsp caster sugar
2 tsp granulated sweetener
1 tsp ground cinnamon
1 tbsp reduced-fat spread, melted

You can't say no to golden, fluffy doughnut holes that are ready in just 15 minutes! Forget the deep fryer and all that messy oil – our ridiculously simple recipe creates a soft, pillowy dough that puffs up beautifully in your trusty air fryer. Make sure to roll them in our cinnamon sugar coating while they're still hot for that perfect sweet and spicy finish. They're proper tasty – and only 39 calories each!

Add the flour, yoghurt, baking powder and vanilla to a bowl. Mix with your hands and bring together into a soft ball of dough.

Divide the dough into 16 and roll into balls. Try not to handle the doughnut holes too much – they don't need to be perfectly round.

Remove the basket from your air fryer and spray the drawer with low-calorie cooking spray. Alternatively, use a silicone liner or tin that fits inside your air fryer basket. Add the doughnut holes and spray again. Air-fry at 180°C for 10 minutes giving them a shake halfway through to get an even golden brown colour.

In a small bowl, combine the sugar, sweetener and cinnamon.

When cooked, pour the melted spread over the doughnut holes and shake. Sprinkle over the cinnamon sugar mixture and toss to coat evenly.

Serve four doughnut holes per person.

TIP:
Per doughnut hole – 39 kcal and 6.7g carbs.

VEGGIE

VEGAN
USE VEGAN ICE CREAM OR YOGHURT

DAIRY FREE
USE DF ICE CREAM OR YOGHURT

GLUTEN FREE
USE GF OATS

EASY TO HALVE
SEE INDEX

CARAMELIZED BAKED APPLES

10 MINS   20 MINS   SERVES 4

PER SERVING:
124 KCAL /21G CARBS

2 apples (we used Granny Smith)
½ tbsp brown granulated sweetener (you can use white if you prefer)
½ tsp ground cinnamon
1½ tbsp low-calorie caramel syrup
30g rolled oats
15g pecans, finely chopped

TO ACCOMPANY *(optional)*:
60g low-calorie vanilla ice cream (+ 62 kcal per serving)

Soft, sweet and perfect for dessert – or even breakfast – these Caramelized Baked Apples are a firm favourite in our kitchen, and we've no doubt they will be in yours, too. All it takes to give the apples their sweet, melt-in-the-mouth texture is a dusting of cinnamon, a drizzle of low-calorie caramel syrup and 15 minutes in your air fryer. Then it's onto your granola topping – a mixture of oats, pecans and the remaining syrup that adds a crunchy texture and even more fibre. Serve on their own or with a dollop of fat-free Greek yoghurt!

Slice the apples in half and scoop out the cores to create a little hollow in each apple half.

In a bowl, combine the sweetener with ¼ teaspoon of the cinnamon.

Brush the cut surfaces of the apples with ½ tablespoon of the caramel syrup and sprinkle over the cinnamon mixture.

Line the air fryer basket with non-stick baking paper and place the apples inside, cut-sides up.

Air-fry at 180°C for 15 minutes, until the apples are softened and turning golden brown.

Meanwhile, combine the oats, pecans, remaining syrup and cinnamon in a bowl and mix. Sprinkle over the apples and cook for a further 5 minutes until crisp and golden.

Serve warm with your choice of accompaniment.

TIP:
Alternatively, you can serve these for breakfast with 50g fat-free Greek yoghurt for an additional 58 kcal.

BLUEBERRY CHEESECAKE SWIRLS

🕐 **10 MINS**   🍲 **10-12 MINS**   ✕ **MAKES 16**

PER SERVING:
89 KCAL /11G CARBS

- 120g reduced-fat cream cheese
- 2 tbsp granulated sweetener
- 100g frozen blueberries, defrosted
- 320g ready-rolled light puff pastry sheet

The best dessert recipes are the ones that are ready in less than 20 minutes and will have your guests hankering for seconds… and even thirds! All you need to make these blueberry cheesecake beauties is four ingredients and your trusty air fryer. The filling can be whipped up in no time at all, then it's simply a case of rolling it into your pastry to create that stunning swirl finish. They're freezer-friendly too, so you can even double the batch for fuss-free two-course meals!

In a bowl, combine the cream cheese and 1 tablespoon of the sweetener and mix until smooth. In another bowl, add the blueberries and remaining sweetener and mix.

Unroll the pastry sheet, leaving it on the paper backing. Spread the cream cheese mixture over the pastry sheet in a thin layer, leaving a 1cm (½in) gap along one long edge.

Spoon the blueberries over the pastry, leaving the 1cm (½in) gap along the long edge clear.

Roll up the pastry tightly, starting with the long edge on the opposite side to the gap and using the paper backing to help you. Keep rolling it up until you have a 'Swiss roll'. When you have finished rolling the pastry, make sure it is seam-side down, then cut it into 16 spiral-shaped slices.

Carefully transfer the slices to the air fryer basket, leaving gaps between each one and pressing the seam on each to ensure a good seal. You may need to do this in batches, depending on the size of your air fryer.

Air-fry at 190°C for 10–12 minutes, turning halfway through, until golden and crisp.

These swirls are best served warm. You can freeze them after baking, just allow them to cool fully and place in a freezer-proof container.

USE DF SPREAD

PEANUT BUTTER COOKIES

⏱ **10 MINS + 20 MINS CHILLING**   🍲 **8-10 MINS**   ✕ **SERVES 16**

PER SERVING:
92 KCAL / 8.8G CARBS

50g reduced-fat spread
30g brown granulated sweetener
30g caster sugar
100g peanut butter
50g self-raising flour
50g oats
½ medium egg, beaten
10g roasted peanuts, finely chopped

Biscuit tin looking a little sparse? Stock it up with these delicious Peanut Butter Cookies. Baked with just eight ingredients and no fancy components to hunt down, they're simple to whip up and will be a hit with the whole family. Or if it's just you and you're not sure you can get through the whole batch right away, you can always freeze for a grab-and-go sweet treat another day! They pair perfectly with your morning cuppa.

Combine the reduced-fat spread, sweetener, sugar and peanut butter in a large mixing bowl. Beat with a wooden spoon until smooth and creamy.

Add the flour and oats and mix again.

Use your hands to bring together into a ball of dough. Divide the dough into 16 pieces and roughly roll into balls. Place onto a lined baking tray. Pop into the fridge for a minimum of 20 minutes.

Press each ball of dough to flatten into a cookie shape. Brush with the beaten egg and sprinkle over the chopped peanuts. Press the nuts lightly into the surface of each cookie.

Line the air fryer drawer with non-stick baking paper and place the cookies into the drawer. You may need to do this in batches, depending on the size of your air fryer.

Bake for 8–10 minutes until lightly golden brown. Leave to cool in the drawer.

TIP:
If you don't have brown sweetener, you can swap for white sweetener, or you can use brown sugar and adjust the calories accordingly.

Freeze or store in an airtight container for up to 4 days.

SLICE AND WRAP PORTIONS INDIVIDUALLY

USE DF SPREAD

PUMPKIN BREAD

🕐 **10 MINS + 30 MINS COOLING**   🍲 **40 MINS**   ✗ **SERVES 10**

PER SERVING:
177 KCAL / 29G CARBS

SPECIAL EQUIPMENT:
450g (1lb) loaf tin

100g reduced-fat spread, melted, plus extra for greasing
200g self-raising flour
½ tsp baking powder
1 tsp ground cinnamon
½ tsp ground nutmeg
½ tsp ground ginger
¼ tsp salt
50g brown sugar (or caster sugar if you prefer)
50g brown granulated sweetener (or white if you prefer)
200g pumpkin puree
2 medium eggs
1 tsp vanilla extract
2 tbsp maple carob syrup
2 tbsp icing sugar

Everyone loves a fluffy banana loaf, and everyone's always looking for pumpkin flavours once the temperatures start to drop, so we've combined the two to come up with this warming Pumpkin Bread. All you need to do is switch out the usual bananas for pumpkin puree – and we've added in some maple syrup to make things extra autumnal. And if you just can't get enough of this spicy flavour, the puree we've used is available all year round.

Grease and line the loaf tin.

Add the dry ingredients to a bowl and mix until combined.

In another bowl, combine the melted spread, pumpkin puree, eggs and vanilla and mix well.

Pour the pumpkin mixture into the dry ingredients and mix well with a wooden spoon until smooth and the ingredients are fully combined.

Scrape the mixture into the prepared tin and roughly smooth out the top.

Place into the air fryer and cook at 150°C for 40 minutes. If the top is getting a little brown, cover with foil and continue to cook until a skewer comes out clean.

Leave to cool in the tin until cool enough to handle, then transfer to a wire rack to cool completely.

In a small bowl, combine the maple syrup and icing sugar and mix until smooth, then drizzle over the loaf, slice and serve!

TIP:
We've used tinned pumpkin puree which is available all year round online or seasonally in the supermarket. Alternatively, you can cook your own pumpkin until soft and mash or blitz until smooth.

We used Clarks Original Maple Syrup with Carob Syrup.

EASY TO HALVE

Breakfasts

CLOUD PANCAKES

1 egg white
1 egg yolk
15g fat-free Greek yoghurt
25ml skimmed milk
1 tsp vanilla extract
30g plain flour
1 tbsp granulated sweetener
1 tbsp caster sugar
low-calorie cooking spray
1 tsp icing sugar
80g strawberries, sliced
50g raspberries
40g blueberries
2 tsp maple syrup

Fakeaways

RANCH BURGERS

125g 5%-fat beef mince
½ tsp garlic granules
½ tsp onion granules
¼ tsp mixed herbs
¼ tsp ground cumin
¼ tsp mustard powder
low-calorie cooking spray
½ onion, peeled and sliced

FOR THE RANCH SAUCE:
1½ tbsp fat-free Greek yoghurt
1 tbsp lighter-than-light mayonnaise
½ tbsp finely chopped fresh chives
½ tbsp finely chopped fresh parsley
⅛ tsp Dijon mustard
½ tsp lemon juice
salt and freshly ground black pepper, to taste

TO SERVE:
2 brioche rolls, approx. 65g each, halved
2 reduced-fat cheese slices
50g gherkins, sliced
½ tomato, sliced
50g lettuce, sliced

CRISPY CAULIFLOWER TACOS

Tip: Leftover mini wraps can be frozen for use another time.

FOR THE PINK PICKLED ONIONS:
½ red onion, peeled and thinly sliced into rings
25ml white wine vinegar
½ tsp granulated sweetener (or sugar)

FOR THE CHEESY SLAW:
75g fat-free Greek yoghurt
50g reduced-fat Cheddar, finely grated
½ tsp English mustard
1½–2 tbsp cold water
90g white cabbage, finely shredded
½ carrot, grated (no need to peel)
1 spring onion, finely sliced

FOR THE TACOS:
1 tbsp self-raising flour
½ tsp garlic granules
½–1 tsp chilli powder
½ tsp ground cumin
½ tsp onion granules
2½ tbsp skimmed milk
½ cauliflower, cut into bite-size florets (about 225g prepared cauliflower)
low-calorie cooking spray
5g panko breadcrumbs
4 mini wraps
½ bag of mixed leaves
salt and freshly ground black pepper, to taste

KATSU COD

low-calorie cooking spray
½ medium onion, peeled and diced
1–2 garlic cloves, peeled and crushed
1 medium carrot, peeled and sliced, plus ¼ carrot cut into ribbons for garnish
125g potato, peeled and chopped
½ tbsp garam masala
½ tbsp mild curry powder
½ tbsp soy sauce
¾ tsp garlic granules
¾ tsp onion granules
175ml vegetable stock (½ vegetable stock cube dissolved in 175ml water)
1 tbsp cornflour
1 medium egg, beaten
25g panko breadcrumbs
175g skinless, boneless cod fillets
½ tbsp white granulated sweetener
salt and freshly ground black pepper, to taste
coriander leaves, to garnish

CHICKEN and COCONUT CURRY

Tip: The leftover coconut milk can be frozen in an airtight container for up to 1 month.

200g chicken breast, diced
½ onion, peeled and diced
½ red pepper, sliced
50g fine green beans, trimmed
low-calorie cooking spray

small piece of root ginger, peeled and grated
2 garlic cloves, peeled and crushed
40g mild curry paste (we used korma)
1 tbsp tomato puree
1 x 200ml tin light coconut milk
juice of ¼ lime
small handful of fresh coriander leaves, roughly chopped
salt and freshly ground black pepper, to taste

CHICKEN and LEMON NOODLES

1 tbsp cornflour
½ tsp garlic granules
½ tsp onion granules
200g chicken breast, cut into chunky strips
low-calorie cooking spray
1 garlic clove, peeled and crushed
1 tbsp soy sauce
½ tbsp honey
1 tbsp granulated sweetener
juice of 1 lemon
¼ tsp ground ginger
75g dried egg noodles
40g broccoli, cut into small florets
40g mangetout, sliced in half lengthways
1 spring onion, finely sliced
1 tsp sesame seeds
salt and freshly ground black pepper, to taste

MEXICAN-STYLE FISH FINGER SANDWICH

Tip: Brush the leftover avocado half with a little lemon juice and keep it covered in the fridge. It should keep for up to 2 days.

FOR THE GUACAMOLE:
½ small avocado
⅛ cucumber, deseeded and grated
juice of ¼ lime
¼ tsp garlic granules
a few fresh coriander leaves, chopped
salt and freshly ground black pepper, to taste

FOR THE FISH FINGERS:
120g basa fillet, or any firm white fish, such as cod, haddock or pollock
½ tbsp plain flour
1 egg, beaten
30g tortilla chips, crushed into fine crumbs
¼ tsp ground cumin
¼–½ tsp chilli powder, mild or hot depending on your taste
salt and freshly ground black pepper, to taste
low-calorie cooking spray

TO SERVE:
2 x 80g ciabatta rolls, cut in half
½ little gem lettuce, shredded

BIRYANI-STYLE TURKEY

low-calorie cooking spray
2 whole cloves
1 cinnamon stick
2 cardamom pods
½ medium onion, peeled and finely diced
2 garlic cloves, peeled and crushed
½ tsp garlic granules
½ tsp ground cumin
½ tsp ground coriander
½ tsp chilli powder
½ tsp paprika
1 tsp garam masala
¼ tsp ground turmeric
¼ tsp ground ginger
175g 2%-fat turkey mince
50g frozen peas
250g pre-cooked microwaveable rice pouch, or 250g cooked rice
50g fat-free Greek yoghurt
½ tbsp mango chutney
20g pumpkin seeds
20g dried cranberries
salt and freshly ground black pepper, to taste

SWEET and SOUR CRISPY TOFU

225g extra-firm tofu, cut into cubes
low-calorie cooking spray
½ tsp garlic granules
½ tsp onion granules
½ tsp smoked paprika
1 tbsp cornflour
½ red onion, peeled and sliced
1 pepper, deseeded and sliced
½ medium carrot, peeled and cut into strips
1–2 garlic cloves, peeled and crushed
50ml pineapple or orange juice
1½ tbsp reduced-sugar-and-salt ketchup
1 tbsp soy sauce (light or dark)
1 tbsp granulated sweetener
1 tbsp rice vinegar
½ tbsp cornflour mixed to a slurry with ½ tbsp cold water
75g fresh pineapple, chopped into chunks

50g sugar snap peas, cut in half
1 spring onion, finely sliced
½ tsp sesame seeds (optional)
salt and freshly ground black pepper, to taste

CRISPY LAMB

Tip: The extra chickpeas can be kept in an airtight container in the fridge for up to 3 days.

½ tsp ground cumin
½ tsp garlic granules
½ tsp smoked paprika
¼ tsp ground cinnamon
⅛ tsp ground turmeric
1 tbsp cornflour
1 medium egg
200g lean lamb steaks, cut into thin strips
low-calorie cooking spray
65g uncooked basmati rice
½ small red onion, peeled and sliced
½ red pepper, deseeded and sliced
½ large carrot, peeled and cut into matchsticks
¼ courgette, cut into batons
juice of ½ large orange
½ tbsp pomegranate molasses
½ tbsp runny honey
½ tbsp balsamic vinegar
½ x 400g tin chickpeas, drained and rinsed
40g pomegranate seeds
salt and freshly ground black pepper, to taste
small handful fresh parsley, chopped

PORK and PARMESAN BURGERS

low-calorie cooking spray
½ small red onion, peeled and finely chopped
1 garlic clove, peeled and crushed
½ tsp finely chopped fresh rosemary
200g 5%-fat pork mince
15g Parmesan, finely grated
50g lighter-than-light mayonnaise
juice of ¼ lemon
salt and freshly ground black pepper, to taste

TO SERVE:
2 x 60g wholemeal rolls
wedge of iceberg lettuce, shredded
1 tomato, sliced

KEFTEDES (CYPRIOT-STYLE MEATBALLS)

Tip: When mixing the meatball ingredients together, add the egg a little at a time until the mix comes together. You might not need it all.

60g potato, raw and unpeeled, grated
250g 5%-fat minced pork
¼ red onion, peeled and finely chopped
1 garlic clove, peeled and crushed
½ tsp ground cinnamon
small handful of flat-leafed parsley, chopped, plus extra for garnish
10g panko breadcrumbs
1 egg, beaten
juice of ¼ lemon
¼ tsp salt
¼ tsp coarsely ground black pepper
1 tsp extra virgin olive oil, for brushing the meatballs
lemon wedges, to serve

FAJITA CRUNCHWRAP

low-calorie cooking spray
150g chicken breast, diced
½ pepper (any colour), deseeded and sliced
½ red onion, peeled and sliced
1 tsp garlic granules
½ tsp ground coriander
½ tsp ground cumin
½ tsp oregano
¼ tsp mild chilli powder
1 tbsp tomato puree
1 tbsp water
2 soft tortilla wraps, approx. 40g per wrap
30g reduced-fat Cheddar, finely grated
salt and freshly ground black pepper, to taste

FOR THE CREAMY SALSA:
60g cherry tomatoes, diced
1 spring onion, sliced
5g fresh coriander, chopped
juice of ½ lime, plus lime wedge to serve
1½ tbsp fat-free Greek yoghurt

SPANISH-STYLE CHICKEN BUTTER BEAN RICE

Tip: Store leftover butter beans in an airtight container in the fridge for up to 3 days.

40g chorizo, diced
½ small onion, peeled and finely chopped
250g chicken breast, diced
2 garlic cloves, peeled and crushed
1 tsp smoked sweet paprika
½ x 400g tin butter beans, rinsed and drained
juice of ½ lemon
50ml chicken stock (½ chicken stock cube dissolved in 50ml boiling water)

50g fine green beans, trimmed and cut in half
1 x 250g microwaveable long grain rice pouch
salt and freshly ground black pepper, to taste
handful of finely chopped fresh parsley, to garnish
lemon wedges, to serve

TEX-MEX TACOS

Tip: The leftover black beans can be frozen in an airtight container for another time.

low-calorie cooking spray
½ medium red onion, peeled and sliced
½ pepper (any colour), deseeded and sliced
1–2 garlic cloves, peeled and crushed
125g 5%-fat beef mince
1 tbsp smoked paprika
½ tsp ground cumin
½ tsp ground coriander
½ tsp garlic granules
½ tsp onion granules
½ tsp oregano
¼ tsp chilli powder
75g passata
1 tbsp tomato puree
½ tsp granulated sweetener
50g tinned black beans, drained and rinsed
salt and freshly ground black pepper, to taste

TO SERVE:
¼ red onion, peeled and finely sliced
1½ tbsp rice vinegar
2 soft tortilla wraps, approx. 40g per wrap
50g reduced-fat Cheddar, finely grated
50g fat-free Greek yoghurt
juice of 1 lime
60g cherry tomatoes, diced
3g fresh coriander, chopped

HOISIN PORK with NOODLES

250g 5%-fat pork mince
3 spring onions, trimmed and sliced
1 tsp sesame oil
2cm (¾in) piece of root ginger, peeled and grated
1 garlic clove, peeled and crushed
½ tsp Chinese 5-spice
½ carrot, peeled and cut into matchsticks
½ red pepper, deseeded and diced
100g dried egg noodles
50g hoisin sauce
1 tbsp soy sauce
juice of ¼ lime

MOROCCAN-STYLE TOFU KEBABS

75g firm tofu
60g tinned chickpeas, drained and rinsed
¼ red onion, peeled and finely diced
¼ red pepper, deseeded and finely diced
½ tsp smoked paprika
½ tsp garlic granules
¼ tsp ground cumin
¼ tsp ground coriander
¼ tsp ground turmeric
¼ tsp mild chilli powder
40g plain flour
salt and freshly ground black pepper, to taste
low-calorie cooking spray
2 tbsp fat-free Greek yoghurt
½ tbsp finely chopped fresh mint, plus a few leaves to serve

MAPLE and BACON MEATBALLS

2 smoked bacon medallions, cut into small dice
2 tsp maple syrup
low-calorie cooking spray
200g 5%-fat pork mince
½ tsp garlic granules
½ tsp paprika
10g panko breadcrumbs
1 tbsp milk
1 egg yolk
½ tsp salt
freshly ground black pepper, to taste

FOR THE SAUCE:
250g passata
½ tsp garlic granules
½ tbsp maple syrup
salt and freshly ground black pepper, to taste

SRIRACHA SALMON with ROASTED PINEAPPLE SALSA

½ tbsp sriracha
½ tbsp honey
juice of ½ lime
¼ tsp garlic granules
2 x 110g skinless salmon fillets
150g fresh pineapple, peeled and cut into 1.5cm (⅝in) slices
½ red pepper, cut in half and deseeded
low-calorie cooking spray
salt and freshly ground black pepper, to taste
2 spring onions, trimmed and sliced
small handful of fresh coriander leaves, chopped

SPICY BEEF and CHICKPEA FLATBREAD

Tip: Store leftover chickpeas in an airtight container in the fridge for up to 3 days.

125g 5%-fat minced beef
½ tsp garam masala
½ tsp garlic granules
½ tsp onion granules
¼ tsp ground cumin
¼ tsp ground coriander
¼ tsp ground ginger
¼ tsp salt
low-calorie cooking spray
½ x 400g tin chickpeas, drained and rinsed

FOR THE MANGO RAITA:
¼ ripe mango, diced
65g fat-free Greek yoghurt
¼ tsp garlic granules
½ tbsp lime juice
¼ red chilli, finely chopped
a few fresh mint leaves, chopped
salt and freshly ground black pepper, to taste

TO SERVE:
2 mini naan breads, approx. 65g each
½ little gem lettuce, shredded
1 tomato, diced
⅛ cucumber, diced
¼ red onion, peeled and sliced
small handful fresh coriander, chopped

CHICKEN CURRY STRUDEL

Tip: You can wrap your leftover pastry back in its non-stick baking paper and pop in the freezer for use another time.

100g cooked chicken breast, cut into small pieces
1 spring onion, trimmed and finely sliced
38g half-fat crème fraîche
¾ tbsp mild curry paste (we used korma)
½ tsp mango chutney
½ x 320g ready-rolled light puff pastry sheet
½ tbsp milk
¼ tsp black onion seeds
salt and freshly ground black pepper, to taste

Bakes and Roasts

CHICKEN and MANGO CHUTNEY TRAYBAKE

Tips: Leftover unheated rice from the microwaveable rice pouch can be kept covered in the fridge for 2–3 days. The remaining chickpeas can also be frozen in a container to use another time.

250g chicken breast, diced
low-calorie cooking spray
½ red onion, peeled and sliced
½ red pepper, deseeded and sliced
50g courgette, cut into batons
1 tbsp curry powder
½ tbsp garlic granules
½ x 400g tin chickpeas, drained and rinsed
½ x 250g microwaveable rice pouch
2 tbsp mango chutney
juice of ½ lime
80g spinach
1½ tbsp fat-free Greek yoghurt
salt and freshly ground pepper, to taste
5g fresh coriander, stalks and leaves, roughly chopped

CHILLI COTTAGE PIE JACKETS

Tip: The extra chopped tomatoes, sweetcorn and kidney beans can be frozen in containers to use another time.

2 baking potatoes, approx. 175g each
125g 5%-fat minced beef
½ medium onion, peeled and diced
½ pepper, deseeded and diced (any colour)
½ carrot, peeled and diced
1 garlic cloves, peeled and crushed
½ x 400g tin chopped tomatoes
1 tbsp tomato puree
½ tbsp Henderson's relish
½ tsp garlic granules
½ tsp onion granules
½ tsp smoked paprika
½ tsp dried oregano
1 tsp mild chilli powder (or hot if you prefer)
¼ tsp ground cumin
75ml boiling water
40g tinned kidney beans, drained and rinsed
40g tinned sweetcorn, drained
40g reduced-fat Cheddar, finely grated
2 tbsp reduced-fat soured cream
2 tsp fresh chives, finely sliced (optional)
salt and freshly ground black pepper, to taste

CREAMY SAUSAGE GNOCCHI

Tip: If you have a large air fryer, use a silicone liner to prevent the sauce drying out. Leftover gnocchi will keep in the fridge for up to 3 days (or see guidelines on packet).

170g low-fat chicken chipolatas (5 chipolatas)
low-calorie cooking spray
50g reduced-fat cream cheese
25g sun-dried tomato paste
100ml water
½ tsp garlic granules
2 spring onions, trimmed and finely sliced
250g fresh gnocchi
a few fresh basil leaves, shredded
6 cherry tomatoes, halved
salt and freshly ground black pepper, to taste

HAM *and* ASPARAGUS CHICKEN

Tip: If you have a large air fryer, use a silicone liner to prevent the sauce from drying out.

2 skinless, boneless chicken breasts, approx. 150g each
1 garlic clove, peeled and crushed
2 slices Parma ham, excess fat removed
2 reduced-fat cheese slices
60g asparagus spears
low-calorie cooking spray

FOR THE CHEESE SAUCE:
200ml skimmed milk
1½ tbsp cornflour, mixed to a slurry with 3 tbsp of the milk
a small pinch of mustard powder
40g reduced-fat Cheddar, finely grated
salt and freshly ground black pepper, to taste

SMOKY HALLOUMI *and* SWEET POTATO BAKE

Tips: You can wrap the remaining halloumi and freeze it for up to a month.

Store the leftover chickpeas in an airtight container in the fridge for up to 3 days.

115g reduced-fat halloumi, cut into 2cm (¾in) dice
250g sweet potatoes, peeled and cut into 2cm (¾in) dice
½ red onion, peeled and sliced
½ green pepper, deseeded and sliced
½ x 400g tin chickpeas, drained and rinsed
low-calorie cooking spray
1 tsp smoked paprika
½ tsp garlic granules
½ tsp dried oregano
5 cherry tomatoes, halved
50g BBQ sauce
salt and freshly ground black pepper, to taste

SUN-DRIED TOMATO CHICKEN BAKE

200g chicken breast, diced
½ tbsp garlic granules
½ tbsp onion granules
½ tbsp smoked paprika
½ tbsp dried oregano
1 tbsp red pesto
1 tbsp sun-dried tomato paste
½ tbsp tomato puree
75ml boiling water
½ red onion, peeled and finely sliced
½ red pepper, deseeded and finely sliced
200g potatoes (no need to peel)
25g reduced-fat cream cheese
25g sun-dried tomatoes, sliced
low-calorie cooking spray

BOLOGNESE POTATO HASH

Tip: The leftover chopped tomatoes from the tin can be frozen in a container to use another time.

250g 5%-fat beef mince
½ medium onion, peeled and finely diced
1 medium carrot, peeled and finely diced
1 celery stick, finely diced
40g mushrooms, finely diced
1 garlic clove, peeled and crushed
½ x 400g tin chopped tomatoes
1 tbsp tomato puree
½ tbsp Henderson's relish
½ tsp mixed herbs
½ tsp garlic granules
½ tsp onion granules
½ tsp granulated sweetener
75ml beef stock (½ beef stock cube dissolved in 75ml boiling water)
salt and freshly ground black pepper, to taste
150g potatoes, peeled and cut into approx. 2cm (¾in) cubes
low-calorie cooking spray

PEA *and* HAM CROQUETTES

375g potatoes, peeled and cut into chunks
125g frozen peas
2 spring onions, trimmed and finely sliced
5g sliced ham, finely chopped
½ tsp garlic granules
½ tbsp green pesto
10g Parmesan, finely grated
28g panko breadcrumbs
low-calorie cooking spray
salt and freshly ground black pepper, to taste

SUMAC CHICKEN with ROASTED VEGETABLES and HERBY COUSCOUS

2 large skinless, boneless chicken thighs, approx. 150g each
½ red onion, peeled and cut into 1cm (½in) wedges
75g butternut squash, peeled and cut into 1cm (½in) fingers
½ red pepper, deseeded and sliced
½ courgette, cut into 1cm (½in) slices
1 garlic clove, peeled and crushed
low-calorie cooking spray
½ lemon, cut into slices

FOR THE MARINADE:
1 tbsp sumac
¼ tsp chilli flakes
½ tsp ground cinnamon
½ tsp ground cumin
1–2 garlic cloves, peeled and crushed
juice of ½ lemon
1 tsp tomato puree

FOR THE HERBY COUSCOUS:
100g couscous
150ml chicken stock (¼ chicken stock cube dissolved in 150ml boiling water)
¼ tsp garlic granules
a few sprigs flat-leafed parsley, chopped
a few fresh mint leaves, chopped
juice of ¼ lemon
salt and freshly ground black pepper, to taste

SAUSAGE, SAGE and ROSEMARY TRAYBAKE

Tip: The extra butter beans can be frozen in a container to use another time.

125g new potatoes, sliced
low-calorie cooking spray
½ medium red onion, peeled and sliced
75g courgette, sliced
4 reduced-fat pork sausages
½ tbsp dried sage
½ tbsp dried rosemary
½ tsp garlic granules
1 tbsp honey
25ml apple juice
½ x 400g tin butter beans, drained and rinsed
100g Tenderstem broccoli, trimmed

ROASTED VEGETABLE PASTA BAKE

1 pepper, deseeded and chopped (any colour)
½ red onion, peeled and chopped
1–2 garlic cloves, peeled
150g courgette, chopped
40g mushrooms, halved
150g tomatoes, halved
80g butternut squash, peeled and cut into small chunks
1 tbsp red pesto
1 tsp dried basil
1 tsp garlic granules
low-calorie cooking spray
40g feta cheese, roughly crumbled
125g pasta (any shape you prefer)
25g reduced-fat Cheddar, finely grated
salt and freshly ground black pepper, to taste

SWEET CHILLI HALLOUMI-STUFFED CHICKEN

Tips: You can wrap the remaining halloumi and freeze it for up to a month.

1 tsp garlic granules
1 tsp onion granules
½ tsp dried oregano
¼ tsp chilli flakes
2 chicken breasts, approx. 125g each
115g reduced-fat halloumi

FOR THE SWEET CHILLI COATING:
1 tsp chilli flakes
½ tbsp honey
2 tsp sriracha
1 tsp rice vinegar
½ tbsp granulated sweetener
salt and freshly ground black pepper, to taste

PESTO CHICKEN TRAYBAKE

250g new potatoes, sliced
2 tbsp reduced-fat green pesto
50g reduced-fat cream cheese
2 chicken breasts, approx. 130g each
4 smoked bacon medallions
low-calorie cooking spray
120g green beans, trimmed
80g asparagus, woody ends removed
50g cherry tomatoes, halved
salt and freshly ground black pepper, to taste

Light Bites

INDIAN-STYLE SWEET POTATO FRIES and RAITA

FOR THE SWEET POTATO FRIES:
2 medium sweet potatoes, peeled and cut into 1.5cm (⅔in) thick fries, approx. 300g
low-calorie cooking spray
½ tbsp mild curry powder
½ tsp garlic granules

FOR THE RAITA:
50g cucumber, deseeded and coarsely grated
75g fat-free Greek yoghurt
5 fresh mint leaves (stalks removed), finely chopped
½ tsp white granulated sweetener
⅛ tsp garlic granules
salt and freshly ground black pepper, to taste

PIZZA CRUMPETS

2 crumpets
2 slices wafer thin ham, diced
1 sun-dried tomato, finely diced
50g reduced-fat mozzarella
freshly ground black pepper, to taste

FOR THE SAUCE:
1 tbsp tomato puree
½ tbsp water
⅛ tsp garlic granules
¼ tsp dried Italian mixed herbs
⅛ tsp granulated sweetener (or sugar)

PERI-PERI CHICKEN NUGGETS

50g fat-free Greek yoghurt
1 tsp dried oregano
1 tsp garlic granules
1 tsp onion granules
½ tsp smoked paprika
½ tsp chilli flakes
¼ tsp ground ginger
160g chicken breast, chopped into 3–4cm (1¼–1½in) pieces
35g panko breadcrumbs
1 tsp peri-peri seasoning
¼ tsp garlic granules
low-calorie cooking spray

FOR THE DIP:
20g fat-free Greek yoghurt
1 tbsp reduced-fat mayonnaise
juice of ½ lime
salt and freshly ground black pepper, to taste

BUFFALO CHICKEN SANDWICH

150g chicken breast, chopped into 5cm (2in) chunks
½ tsp garlic granules
½ tsp onion granules
½ tsp paprika
½ tbsp buffalo hot sauce
30g reduced-fat cream cheese
15g Stilton
½ tsp honey
25g red cabbage, finely shredded
½ medium carrot, peeled and cut into matchsticks
20g gherkins, sliced into strips
½ stick celery, diced
1 tbsp pickling vinegar, from the jar of gherkins
50g fat-free Greek yoghurt
salt and freshly ground black pepper, to taste
2 brioche rolls, sliced in half

CRISPY CHILLI POTATO SALAD

250g new potatoes, sliced in half
low-calorie cooking spray
50g fat-free Greek yoghurt
½ tbsp rice vinegar
1 tbsp honey
½ tbsp sriracha
¼ tbsp garlic granules
¼ tbsp chilli flakes
1 tbsp reduced-fat mayonnaise
½ red chilli, deseeded and finely diced
salt and freshly ground black pepper, to taste

SPICED CAULIFLOWER and CRANBERRY COUSCOUS

125g cauliflower, cut into bite-size pieces
low-calorie cooking spray
1 tsp garlic granules
½ tsp ground coriander
½ tsp ground cumin
½ tsp smoked paprika
¼ tsp ground turmeric
½ x 400g tin chickpeas, drained and rinsed
50g giant couscous
35g fat-free Greek yoghurt
juice of ¼ lemon
1 tsp honey
¼ tsp sriracha
20g reduced-fat feta cheese, crumbled
10g dried cranberries
salt and freshly ground black pepper, to taste

EASY TO HALVE

ROASTED TOMATO *and* GARLIC SOUP

FOR THE CROUTONS:
½ x 60g wholemeal bread roll
low-calorie cooking spray
¼ tsp garlic granules
8g Parmesan, finely grated

FOR THE SOUP:
6 salad tomatoes, around 425g in total
3 garlic cloves, peeled
low-calorie cooking spray
200ml vegetable stock (½ vegetable stock cube dissolved in 200ml boiling water)
½ tbsp tomato puree
½ tsp balsamic vinegar
a small handful of fresh basil leaves
salt and freshly ground black pepper, to taste

Sweet Treats

CARAMELIZED BAKED APPLES

1 apple (we used Granny Smith)
¾ tsp brown granulated sweetener (you can use white if you prefer)
¼ tsp ground cinnamon
¾ tbsp low-calorie caramel syrup
15g rolled oats
8g pecans, finely chopped

NUTRITIONAL INFO

BREAKFAST	ENERGY KJ/KCAL	FAT (G)	SATURATED FAT (G)	CARBS (G)	SUGAR (G)	FIBRE (G)	PROTEIN (G)
CHERRY COTTAGE CHEESE TOAST	926/219	2.9	1	34	18	2.5	12
CHEESY BEANS AND SOLDIERS	1408/334	6.7	3.2	43	13	10	19
MAPLE, DATE AND TAHINI GRANOLA	827/198	8.9	1.4	23	7.9	3.4	5.5
EGGY BREAD TOASTIE	1664/397	15	6.2	34	3.5	4.5	28
PESTO EGG BAGELS	1286/307	14	4.3	27	4.8	2.2	16
CLOUD PANCAKES	709/168	2.1	0.5	31	18	3.3	5.7
MAPLE PECAN PLAIT	776/186	11	2.5	18	3.7	1.1	3.7
PEANUT BUTTER AND BANANA TOAST	1430/341	14	3.1	40	22	4.4	11
RED PEPPER EGG BITES	364/87	4.7	1.7	1.6	1.3	0.5	9.4

FAKEAWAYS	ENERGY KJ/KCAL	FAT (G)	SATURATED FAT (G)	CARBS (G)	SUGAR (G)	FIBRE (G)	PROTEIN (G)
RANCH BURGERS	1668/396	12	5.7	42	15	3.9	29
CRISPY CAULIFLOWER TACOS	2011/478	14	7	59	14	8.6	26
KATSU COD	1150/273	4.1	1.1	35	7.3	5.7	22
CHICKEN AND COCONUT CURRY	1170/280	13	6.9	11	8.1	4.8	27
CHICKEN AND LEMON NOODLES	1325/313	3.5	0.7	39	7.9	4.3	31
ASIAN-STYLE FISH PARCELS	538/127	1	0.2	8	6.6	3.1	20
MEXICAN-STYLE FISH FINGER SANDWICH	1909/454	15	3.1	52	3.7	5.3	25
BIRYANI-STYLE TURKEY	1943/461	9.8	1.8	56	12	6.3	34
SWEET AND SOUR CRISPY TOFU	1295/309	12	1.7	27	16	7.4	22
CHILLI BEEF KOFTA	2012/476	6.8	3	54	18	6.7	46
BEEF AND MUSHROOM CHOW MEIN	1768/420	9.8	2.5	47	10	6.9	32

FAKEAWAYS	ENERGY KJ/KCAL	FAT (G)	SATURATED FAT (G)	CARBS (G)	SUGAR (G)	FIBRE (G)	PROTEIN (G)
CRISPY LAMB	2081/494	11	4.1	63	20	7.4	31
PORK AND PARMESAN BURGERS	1627/385	7.3	2.8	30	5.5	4.7	47
KEFTEDES (CYPRIOT-STYLE MEATBALLS)	1121/267	10	1.4	12	2.2	2.5	31
FAJITA CRUNCHWRAP	1383/328	8.7	3.3	27	9.1	4.9	31
SPANISH-STYLE CHICKEN BUTTER BEAN RICE	2006/476	11	3.5	46	3.6	9	43
TEX-MEX TACOS	1713/407	12	5.6	36	14	8	32
HOISIN PORK WITH NOODLES	1898/450	7.7	1.8	50	13	6.6	42
MOROCCON-STYLE TOFU KEBABS	893/212	4.4	0.7	25	4	4.8	16
MAPLE AND BACON MEATBALLS	2010/479	17	7.7	31	8	5.7	48
SRIRACHA SALMON WITH ROASTED PINEAPPLE SALSA	1293/306	6.4	1.8	19	14	3.2	39
SPICY BEEF AND CHICKPEA FLATBREAD	1794/425	8	2.1	53	11	10	29
CHICKEN CURRY STRUDEL	1884/449	19	8	44	4.4	3	24

BAKES & ROASTS	ENERGY KJ/KCAL	FAT (G)	SATURATED FAT (G)	CARBS (G)	SUGAR (G)	FIBRE (G)	PROTEIN (G)
CHICKEN AND MANGO CHUTNEY TRAYBAKE	1812/428	4.3	0.8	49	17	7.8	43
CHILLI COTTAGE PIE JACKETS	1959/466	13	7.1	52	14	10	29
CREAMY SAUSAGE GNOCCHI	1643/390	12	3.8	41	5.9	3.6	28
HAM AND ASPARAGUS CHICKEN	1660/394	11	5.3	20	6.6	0.9	54
AUBERGINE PARMIGIANA	1602/383	16	5.4	34	24	11	17
SMOKY HALLOUMI AND SWEET POTATO BAKE	1689/402	13	7.8	42	26	10	23
BEETROOT AND FETA TART	1923/458	18	8.2	55	16	4.2	18
SUN-DRIED TOMATO CHICKEN BAKE	1711/409	17	3.1	29	8.1	7.5	30
BOLOGNESE POTATO HASH	1280/304	5.9	2.8	27	11	5.7	32

BAKES & ROASTS	ENERGY KJ/KCAL	FAT (G)	SATURATED FAT (G)	CARBS (G)	SUGAR (G)	FIBRE (G)	PROTEIN (G)
PEA AND HAM CROQUETTES	1377/327	6	1.9	49	6.4	7.4	16
HUMMUS-CRUSTED CHICKEN	1068/254	7.6	1.1	5.9	1	2.7	38
HARISSA MARMALADE SALMON	1931/461	19	3.5	42	38	6.8	26
STEAK BITES AND POTATOES	1796/427	11	5.6	35	5.7	7.1	46
SUMAC CHICKEN WITH ROASTED VEGETABLES AND HERBY COUSCOUS	1794/425	6.5	1.6	46	8.3	8.1	40
SAUSAGE, SAGE AND ROSEMARY TRAYBAKE	1774/423	16	5.4	37	16	11	27
ROASTED VEGETABLE PASTA BAKE	1906/453	13	5.5	60	15	8.1	19
SESAME AND GINGER COD	786/187	6.7	1.1	6.8	5.9	2.5	24
SWEET CHILLI HALLOUMI STUFFED CHICKEN	1372/326	12	7.8	11	7.7	1.1	45
PESTO CHICKEN TRAYBAKE	1887/449	13	4	24	5.9	5.9	54

LIGHT BITES	ENERGY KJ/KCAL	FAT (G)	SATURATED FAT (G)	CARBS (G)	SUGAR (G)	FIBRE (G)	PROTEIN (G)
INDIAN-STYLE SWEET POTATO FRIES AND RAITA	734/173	1	0.2	33	10	3.9	6.4
COCONUT SALMON BITES	1428/343	23	6.1	7.6	3	1.7	24
BRIE AND HONEY DOUGH BALLS	365/87	2.1	1.2	13	2.2	0.7	3.2
CHILLI CHEESE SLICES	954/228	12	6.6	20	2	1.6	8.3
PIZZA CRUMPETS	754/179	5.1	2.3	21	2.8	2	11
PERI-PERI CHICKEN NUGGETS	870/206	5.3	1	13	2.8	1.3	25
FRUIT AND VEGETABLE CRISPS AND DIPS – VEGETABLES	568/136	4	1	15	11	6	6.7
FRUIT AND VEGETABLE CRISPS AND DIPS – FRUIT	504/120	2.7	1.5	19	17	2.6	4.4
BUFFALO CHICKEN SANDWICH	1764/419	13	6.6	43	14	3.8	31
CRISPY CHILLI POTATO SALAD	764/181	3.4	0.3	30	12	2.7	5.6
CAJUN-STYLE STEAK SALAD	1801/428	14	6.6	24	11	4.6	48

LIGHT BITES	ENERGY KJ/KCAL	FAT (G)	SATURATED FAT (G)	CARBS (G)	SUGAR (G)	FIBRE (G)	PROTEIN (G)
SPROUT AND TAHINI SALAD	1131/273	18	2.4	9.1	5.7	10	13
ASPARAGUS, BROCCOLI AND FETA SALAD	1130/270	11	4.6	9	7.3	9.5	29
SPICED CAULIFLOWER AND CRANBERRY COUSCOUS	814/193	2.7	1	28	8	5.9	12
ROASTED TOMATO AND GARLIC SOUP	508/121	2.7	1.1	15	7.8	3.5	5.1

SWEET TREATS	ENERGY KJ/KCAL	FAT (G)	SATURATED FAT (G)	CARBS (G)	SUGAR (G)	FIBRE (G)	PROTEIN (G)
APRICOT TARTE TATIN	829/199	12	6.2	26	12	1.3	1.8
COOKIE DOUGH POTS	1063/254	13	3.7	37	11	1.9	5.1
CASHEW MACAROONS	211/51	4	0.8	1.6	0.6	0.5	1.9
CHOCOLATE AND BEETROOT MUFFINS	529/126	5	1.7	17	3.7	1.3	4.4
BISCOFF AND BANANA CAKES	807/193	11	2.4	24	98	0.7	2.9
CINNAMON DOUGHNUT HOLES	653/154	2.6	0.6	27	3.9	1.5	6
CARAMELIZED BAKED APPLES	519/124	3.7	0.4	21	14	2.3	1.8
BLUEBERRY CHEESECAKE SWIRLS	375/89	3.9	1.9	11	0.7	0.7	2.4
PEANUT BUTTER COOKIES	384/92	5.9	1.4	8.8	2.3	0.8	2.5
PUMPKIN BREAD	744/177	7.4	1.7	29	8.8	1.2	3.5

INDEX

Note: page numbers in **bold** refer to photos.

air fryers 6, 9–11
    accessories 22–3
    baskets, drawers and shelves 10–11, 22
    choice of 22
    cleaning and care 11
    cooking functions 10
    cooking guide 30–1
    energy efficiency 9
    how they work 9
    preheat settings 10
    temperatures 10
    wattage/power 10
apple
    caramelized baked apples 190, **191**
    fruit crisps and dips 159, **160–1**
apricot tarte tatin 178, **179**
asparagus
    asparagus, broccoli and feta salad 170, **171**
    ham and asparagus chicken 110–11, **111**, 205
    pesto chicken traybake 140, **141**, 206–7
aubergine parmigiana **112**, 113
avocado, guacamole 68, **69**, 201

bacon
    cooking guide 31
    maple and bacon meatballs **94**, 95, 203
    pesto chicken traybake 140, **141**, 206–7
bagels, pesto egg 42, **43**
bakes 103–40, 204–7
baking powder 20
balsamic vinegar 78, 116, 174, 202, 208
banana
    Biscoff and banana cakes 186, **187**
    peanut butter and banana toast 50, **51**
basa, Mexican-style fish finger sandwich 68, **69**, 201
basil 42, 108, 113, 148, 205
beans 17
    asparagus, broccoli and feta salad 170, **171**
    cheesy beans and soldiers 36, **37**
    chilli cottage pie jackets 106, **107**, 204–5
    sausage, sage and rosemary traybake 132, **133**, 206
    Spanish-style chicken butter bean rice 86, **87**, 202–3
    Tex-Mex tacos 88, **89**, 203
    see also green bean
beef
    beef and mushroom chow mein 76, **77**
    Bolognese potato hash 120, **121**, 205
    Cajun-style steak salad 166, **167**
    chilli beef kofta 74, **75**
    chilli cottage pie jackets 106, **107**, 204–5
    ranch burgers 56, **57**, 200
    spicy beef and chickpea flatbread 98, **99**, 204
    steak bites and potatoes 128, **129**
    Tex-Mex tacos 88, **89**, 203
beetroot
    beetroot and feta tart 116, **117**
    chocolate and beetroot muffins **184**, 185
biryani-style turkey 70, **71**, 201
Biscoff and banana cakes 186, **187**
blueberry
    blueberry cheesecake swirls 192, 193, **194–5**, 200
    cloud pancakes 44–5, **45**, 200
Bolognese potato hash 120, **121**, 205
bread (ready-made) 18
    cheesy beans and soldiers 36, **37**
    croutons 166, **167**, 174, **175**, 208
    eggy bread toastie 40, **41**
    Mexican-style fish finger sandwich 68, **69**, 201
    pork and Parmesan burgers 80, **81**, 202
    spicy beef and chickpea 98, **99**, 204
    see also brioche rolls (ready-made); pitta bread (ready-made); toast
breadcrumbs
    aubergine parmigiana **112**, 113
    see also panko breadcrumbs
breakfasts 33–52, 200
brie and honey dough balls 148–9, **149–51**
brioche rolls (ready-made)
    buffalo chicken sandwich 162, **163**, 207
    ranch burgers 56, **57**, 200
broccoli 64, 169, 201
    see also Tenderstem broccoli
Brussel's sprout and tahini salad **168**, 169
buffalo chicken sandwich 162, **163**, 207

burgers
    pork and Parmesan burgers 80, **81**, 202
    ranch burgers 56, **57**, 200
butter bean 132, 206
    Spanish-style chicken butter bean rice **86**, 87, 202–3
butternut squash
    roasted vegetable pasta bake 134, **135**, 206
    sumac chicken with roasted vegetables and herby couscous 130–1, **131**, 206

cabbage (red), buffalo chicken sandwich 162, **163**, 207
Cajun-style steak salad 166, **167**
cakes
    Biscoff and banana cakes 186, **187**
    pumpkin bread 198, **199**
carrot
    Asian-style fish parcels 66, **67**
    Bolognese potato hash 120, **121**, 205
    buffalo chicken sandwich 162, **163**, 207
    chilli cottage pie jackets 106, **107**, 204–5
    crispy cauliflower tacos 58, **59**, 200
    crispy lamb 78–9, **79**, 202
    harissa marmalade salmon **126**, 127
    hoisin pork with noodles 90, **91**, 203
    katsu cod 60, **61**, 200
    sweet and sour crispy tofu 72, **73**, 201–2
    vegetable crisps and dips 158, **160**–1
cashew nut
    cashew macaroons 182, **183**
    maple, date and tahini granola 38, **39**
cauliflower
    crispy cauliflower tacos 58, **59**, 200
    spiced cauliflower and cranberry couscous 172, **173**, 207
celery 120, 162, 205, 207
Cheddar
    cheese sauce 110–11, **111**, 205
    cheesy beans and soldiers 36, **37**
    chilli cottage pie jackets 106, **107**, 204–5
    crispy cauliflower tacos 58, **59**, 200
    eggy bread toastie **40**, 41
    fajita crunchwrap 84, **85**, 202
    pesto egg bagels 42, **43**
    roasted vegetable pasta bake 134, **135**, 206
    Tex-Mex tacos 88, **89**, 203
cheese
    aubergine parmigiana **112**, 113
    brie and honey dough balls 148–9, **149**–51

buffalo chicken sandwich 162, **163**, 207
cheese sauce 110–11, **111**, 205
cheesy beans and soldiers 36, **37**
cheesy slaw 58, **59**, 200
chilli cheese slices 152, **153**
dressing 166, **167**
ham and asparagus chicken 110–11, **111**, 205
pizza crumpets 154, **155**, 207
ranch burgers 56, **57**, 200
see also Cheddar; cottage cheese; cream cheese; feta; halloumi; Parmesan
cheesecake, blueberry cheesecake swirls **192**, 193, **194**–5
cherry cottage cheese toast 34, **35**
chicken
    buffalo chicken sandwich 162, **163**, 207
    chicken and coconut curry **62**, 63, 201
    chicken curry strudel 100, **101**, 204
    chicken and lemon noodles 64, **65**, 201
    chicken and mango chutney traybake 104, **105**, 204
    cooking guide 31
    creamy sausage gnocchi 108, **109**, 205
    fajita crunchwrap 84, **85**, 202
    ham and asparagus chicken 110–11, **111**, 205
    hummus-crusted chicken 124, **125**
    peri-peri chicken nuggets 156, **157**, 207
    pesto chicken traybake 140, **141**, 206–7
    Spanish-style chicken butter bean rice **86**, 87, 202–3
    sumac chicken with roasted vegetables and herby couscous 130–1, **131**, 206
    sun-dried tomato chicken bake 118, **119**, 205
    sweet chilli halloumi stuffed chicken 138, **139**, 206
chickpea
    chicken and mango chutney traybake 104, **105**, 204
    crispy lamb 78–9, **79**, 202
    Moroccan-style tofu kebabs 92, **93**, 203
    smoky halloumi and sweet potato bake 114, **115**, 205
    spiced cauliflower and cranberry couscous 172, **173**, 207
    spicy beef and chickpea flatbread 98, **99**, 204
chilli
    chilli beef kofta 74, **75**
    chilli cheese slices 152, **153**
    chilli cottage pie jackets 106, **107**, 204–5
    crispy chilli potato salad 164, **165**, 207

sweet chilli halloumi stuffed chicken **138**, 139, 206
chives 106, 164, 200, 204–5, 207
chocolate
    chocolate and beetroot muffins **184**, 185
    cookie dough pots 180, **181**
    peanut butter and banana toast 50, **51**
chorizo, Spanish-style chicken butter bean rice **86**, 87, 202–3
chow mein, beef and mushroom 76, **77**
ciabatta rolls, Mexican-style fish finger sandwich 68, **69**, 201
cinnamon
    caramelized baked apples 190, **191**
    cinnamon doughnut holes 188, **189**
    fruit crisps and dips 159, **160–1**
    keftedes 82, **83**, 202
    maple, date and tahini granola 38, **39**
    maple plant plait 46, **47–9**
    pumpkin bread 198, **199**
cloud pancakes 44–5, **45**, 200
coconut
    chicken and coconut curry **62**, 63, 201
    coconut salmon bites 146, **147**
cod
    katsu cod 60, **61**, 200
    sesame and ginger cod 136, **137**
conversion charts 28
cookie dough pots 180, **181**
cookies, peanut butter 196, **197**
coriander (fresh) 60, 63, 66, 68, 84, 88, 98, 104, 152, 166, 200–4
cottage cheese
    cherry cottage cheese toast 34, **35**
    red pepper egg bites 52, **53**
    vegetable crisps and dips 158, **160–1**
courgette
    Asian-style fish parcels 66, **67**
    chicken and mango chutney traybake 104, **105**, 204
    crispy lamb 78–9, **79**, 202
    roasted vegetable pasta bake 134, **135**, 206
    sausage, sage and rosemary traybake 132, **133**, 206
    sumac chicken with roasted vegetables and herby couscous 130–1, **131**, 206
couscous
    herby couscous 130–1, **131**, 206
    spiced cauliflower and cranberry couscous 172, **173**, 207

cranberry
    biryani-style turkey **70**, 71, 201
    spiced cauliflower and cranberry couscous 172, **173**, 207
cream cheese
    blueberry cheesecake swirls **192**, 193, **194–5**
    buffalo chicken sandwich 162, **163**, 207
    creamy sausage gnocchi 108, **109**, 205
    fruit crisps and dips 159, **160–1**
    pesto chicken traybake 140, **141**, 206–7
    pesto egg bagels 42, **43**
    steak bites and potatoes 128, **129**
    sun-dried tomato chicken bake 118, **119**, 205
crisps
    fruit crisps and dips 159, **160–1**
    vegetable crisps and dips 158, **160–1**
croquettes, pea and ham 122, **123**, 206
croutons 166, **167**, 174, **175**, 208
crumpets, pizza 154, **155**, 207
crunchwrap, fajita 84, **85**, 202
cucumber
    chilli beef kofta 74, **75**
    guacamole 68, **69**, 201
    raita 144, **145**, 207
    spicy beef and chickpea flatbread 98, **99**, 204
curry
    chicken and coconut curry **62**, 63, 201
    chicken curry strudel 100, **101**, 204

dairy, reduced-fat 17
date, tahini and maple granola 38, **39**
dips 156, **157**, 158–9, **160–1**, 207
dough balls, brie and honey 148–9, **149–51**
doughnut holes, cinnamon 188, **189**
dressings 166, **167**
dried fruit 21, 71, 201
    see also specific dried fruit

egg 18
    beetroot and feta tart 116, **117**
    Biscoff and banana cakes 186, **187**
    cashew macaroons 182, **183**
    chilli cheese slices 152, **153**
    chocolate and beetroot muffins **184**, 185
    cloud pancakes 44–5, **45**, 200
    cookie dough pots 180, **181**
    crispy lamb 78–9, **79**, 202
    eggy bread toastie **40**, 41
    katsu cod 60, **61**, 200
    keftedes 82, **83**, 202

maple and bacon meatballs **94**, 95, 203
maple plant plait 46, **47–9**
Mexican-style fish finger sandwich 68, **69**, 201
peanut butter cookies 196, **197**
pesto egg bagels 42, **43**
pumpkin bread 198, **199**
red pepper egg bites 52, **53**
equipment 22–6

fajita crunchwrap 84, **85**, 202
fakeaways 55–101, 200–4
fats, cooking 18
feta
  asparagus, broccoli and feta salad 170, **171**
  beetroot and feta tart 116, **117**
  red pepper egg bites 52, **53**
  roasted vegetable pasta bake 134, **135**, 206
  spiced cauliflower and cranberry couscous 172, **173**, 207
fish
  Asian-style fish parcels 66, **67**
  coconut salmon bites 146, **147**
  cooking guide 31
  harissa marmalade salmon **126**, 127
  katsu cod 60, **61**, 200
  Mexican-style fish finger sandwich 68, **69**, 201
  sesame and ginger cod 136, **137**
  sriracha salmon with roasted pineapple salsa 96, **97**, 203–4
flatbread, spicy beef and chickpea 98, **99**, 204
flours 20
freezable recipes 14
freezing guidelines 15
fries, Indian-style sweet potato fries and raita 144, **145**, 207
frozen fruit/vegetables 17
fruit 21
  frozen 17
  fruit crisps and dips 159, **160–1**
  tinned 21
  see also dried fruit; *specific fruit*

garlic, roasted tomato and garlic soup 174, **175**, 208
gherkins 56, 162, 200, 207
ginger
  Asian-style fish parcels 66, **67**
  chicken and coconut curry **62**, 63, 201
  pumpkin bread 198, **199**
  sesame and ginger cod 136, **137**

glaze 74, **75**
gluten-free recipes 14
gnocchi, creamy sausage 108, **109**, 205
granola, maple, date and tahini 38, **39**
Greek yoghurt
  asparagus, broccoli and feta salad 170, **171**
  biryani-style turkey **70**, 71, 201
  buffalo chicken sandwich 162, **163**, 207
  chicken and mango chutney traybake 104, **105**, 204
  chilli beef kofta 74, **75**
  chocolate and beetroot muffins **184**, 185
  cinnamon doughnut holes 188, **189**
  cloud pancakes 44–5, **45**, 200
  creamy salsa 84, **85**, 202
  crispy cauliflower tacos 58, **59**, 200
  crispy chilli potato salad 164, **165**, 207
  dips 156, **157**, 207
  dressings 166, **167**
  fruit crisps and dips 159, **160–1**
  keftedes 82, **83**, 202
  mango raita 98, **99**, 204
  Moroccan-style tofu kebabs 92, **93**, 203
  peri-peri chicken nuggets 156, **157**, 207
  raita 144, **145**, 207
  ranch sauce 56, **57**, 200
  spiced cauliflower and cranberry couscous 172, **173**, 207
  Tex-Mex tacos 88, **89**, 203
green bean
  chicken and coconut curry **62**, 63, 201
  harissa marmalade salmon **126**, 127
  pesto chicken traybake 140, **141**, 206–7
  Spanish-style chicken butter bean rice **86**, 87, 202–3
  steak bites and potatoes 128, **129**
guacamole 68, **69**, 201

halloumi
  smoky halloumi and sweet potato bake 114, **115**, 205
  sweet chilli halloumi stuffed chicken 138, **139**, 206
ham
  eggy bread toastie **40**, 41
  ham and asparagus chicken 110–11, **111**, 205
  pea and ham croquettes 122, **123**, 206
  pizza crumpets 154, **155**, 207
harissa marmalade salmon **126**, 127
hash, Bolognese potato 120, **121**, 205

herbs 16
    herby couscous 130–1, **131**, 206
high protein recipes 14
hoisin pork with noodles 90, **91**, 203
honey
    brie and honey dough balls 148–9, **149–51**
    cherry cottage cheese toast 34, **35**
    glaze 74, **75**
hummus-crusted chicken 124, **125**

icing 46, **47–9**
ingredients, key 16–21

katsu cod 60, **61**, 200
kebabs, Moroccan-style tofu 92, **93**, 203
keftedes (Cypriot-style meatballs) 82, **83**, 202
kidney bean, chilli cottage pie jackets 106, **107**, 204–5
kit 22–6
knives 23
kofta, chilli beef 74, **75**

lamb, crispy 78–9, **79**, 202
lemon and chicken noodles 64, **65**, 201
lettuce 56, 80, 98, 200, 202, 204
light bites 143–74, 207–8
lime
    chicken and mango chutney traybake 104, **105**, 204
    creamy salsa 84, **85**, 202
    dip 156, **157**, 207

macaroons, cashew 182, **183**
mango chutney (ready-made)
    chicken curry strudel 100, **101**, 204
    chicken and mango chutney traybake 104, **105**, 204
mango raita 98, **99**, 204
maple syrup
    cloud pancakes 44–5, **45**, 200
    fruit crisps and dips 159, **160–1**
    maple, date and tahini granola 38, **39**
    maple and bacon meatballs 94, **95**, 203
    maple plant plait 46, **47–9**
    peanut butter and banana toast 50, **51**
marinade, sumac 130–1, **131**, 206
marmalade harissa salmon 126, **127**
mayo (ready-made)
    coconut salmon bites 146, **147**
    crispy chilli potato salad 164, **165**, 207
    dip 156, **157**, 207
    pork and Parmesan burgers 80, **81**, 202
    ranch sauce 56, **57**, 200
meatballs
    keftedes (Cypriot-style meatballs) 82, **83**, 202
    maple and bacon meatballs 94, **95**, 203
mint
    cherry cottage cheese toast 34, **35**
    herby couscous 130–1, **131**, 206
    mango raita 98, **99**, 204
    Moroccan-style tofu kebabs 92, **93**, 203
    raita 144, **145**, 207
mozzarella
    aubergine parmigiana **112**, 113
    pizza crumpets 154, **155**, 207
muffins, chocolate and beetroot **184**, 185
mushroom
    beef and mushroom chow mein 76, **77**
    Bolognese potato hash 120, **121**, 205
    roasted vegetable pasta bake 134, **135**, 206

naan bread (pre-made), spicy beef and chickpea flatbread 98, **99**, 204
noodles 20
    beef and mushroom chow mein 76, **77**
    chicken and lemon noodles 64, **65**, 201
    hoisin pork with noodles 90, **91**, 203
nuts 20
    see also specific nuts

oats 20
    caramelized baked apples 190, **191**
    maple, date and tahini granola 38, **39**
    peanut butter cookies 196, **197**
oils, low-calorie spray 18
onion, pink pickled 58, **59**, 200
ovens, conventional 9, 28

pak choi 66, 76, 136
pancakes, cloud 44–5, **45**, 200
panko breadcrumbs
    coconut salmon bites 146, **147**
    crispy cauliflower tacos 58, **59**, 200
    katsu cod 60, **61**, 200
    keftedes 82, **83**, 202
    maple and bacon meatballs 94, **95**, 203
    pea and ham croquettes 122, **123**, 206
    peri-peri chicken nuggets 156, **157**, 207
pans 23
Parmesan
    croutons 174, **175**, 208

pea and ham croquettes 122, **123**, 206
pork and Parmesan burgers 80, **81**, 202
parsley 56, 78–9, 82, 87, 130–1, 200, 202–3, 206
passata
    cheesy beans and soldiers 36, **37**
    maple and bacon meatballs **94**, 95, 203
    Tex-Mex tacos 88, **89**, 203
pasta 20
    roasted vegetable pasta bake 134, **135**, 206
    tomato sauce for maple and bacon meatballs **94**, 95, 203
pastry 18
    see also puff pastry (ready-rolled)
peanut butter
    peanut butter and banana toast 50, **51**
    peanut butter cookies 196, **197**
pear, fruit crisps and dips 159, **160–1**
peas
    biryani-style turkey **70**, 71, 201
    pea and ham croquettes 122, **123**, 206
pecan nut
    caramelized baked apples 190, **191**
    maple plant plait 46, **47–9**
    sprout and tahini salad **168**, 169
pepper
    beef and mushroom chow mein 76, **77**
    Cajun-style steak salad 166, **167**
    chicken and coconut curry **62**, 63, 201
    chicken and mango chutney traybake 104, **105**, 204
    chilli cottage pie jackets 106, **107**, 204–5
    crispy lamb 78–9, **79**, 202
    fajita crunchwrap 84, **85**, 202
    hoisin pork with noodles 90, **91**, 203
    Moroccan-style tofu kebabs 92, **93**, 203
    red pepper egg bites 52, **53**
    roasted vegetable pasta bake 134, **135**, 206
    smoky halloumi and sweet potato bake 114, **115**, 205
    sriracha salmon with roasted pineapple salsa 96, **97**, 203–4
    sumac chicken with roasted vegetables and herby couscous 130–1, **131**, 206
    sun-dried tomato chicken bake 118, **119**, 205
    sweet and sour crispy tofu 72, **73**, 201–2
    Tex-Mex tacos 88, **89**, 203
peri-peri chicken nuggets 156, **157**, 207
pesto (ready-made)
    pea and ham croquettes 122, **123**, 206
    pesto chicken traybake 140, **141**, 206–7

pesto egg bagels 42, **43**
roasted vegetable pasta bake 134, **135**, 206
pickled onion, pink 58, **59**, 200
pineapple
    roasted pineapple salsa 96, **97**, 203–4
    sweet and sour crispy tofu 72, **73**, 201–2
pitta bread (ready-made), chilli beef kofta 74, **75**
pizza crumpets 154, **155**, 207
pomegranate seed, crispy lamb 78–9, **79**, 202
pork
    hoisin pork with noodles 90, **91**, 203
    keftedes 82, **83**, 202
    maple and bacon meatballs **94**, 95, 203
    pork and Parmesan burgers 80, **81**, 202
potato 18
    Bolognese potato hash 120, **121**, 205
    chilli cottage pie jackets 106, **107**, 204–5
    cooking guide 31
    crispy chilli potato salad 164, **165**, 207
    katsu cod 60, **61**, 200
    keftedes 82, **83**, 202
    pea and ham croquettes 122, **123**, 206
    pesto chicken traybake 140, **141**, 206–7
    sausage, sage and rosemary traybake 132, **133**, 206
    steak bites and potatoes 128, **129**
    sun-dried tomato chicken bake 118, **119**, 205
protein 16
puff pastry (ready-rolled)
    apricot tarte tatin 178, **179**
    beetroot and feta tart 116, **117**
    blueberry cheesecake swirls 192, **193**, **194–5**
    chicken curry strudel 100, **101**, 204
    chilli cheese slices 152, **153**
    maple plant plait 46, **47–9**
pulses 17
pumpkin bread 198, **199**
pumpkin seed
    biryani-style turkey **70**, 71, 201
    maple, date and tahini granola 38, **39**

raita 144, **145**, 207
    mango raita 98, **99**, 204
ranch burgers 56, **57**, 200
raspberry, cloud pancakes 44–5, **45**, 200
reheating guidelines 15
rice 17
    Asian-style fish parcels 66, **67**
    biryani-style turkey **70**, 71, 201
    chicken and coconut curry **62**, 63, 201

chicken and mango chutney traybake 104, **105**, 204
crispy lamb 78–9, **79**, 202
katsu cod 60, **61**, 200
microwaveable rice 20
sesame and ginger cod 136, **137**
Spanish-style chicken butter bean rice **86**, 87, 202–3
sriracha salmon with roasted pineapple salsa 96, **97**, 203–4
sweet and sour crispy tofu 72, **73**, 201–2
roasts 103–40, 204–7

salad leaves
aubergine parmigiana **112**, 113
beetroot and feta tart 116, **117**
Bolognese potato hash 120, **121**, 205
chicken curry strudel 100, **101**, 204
chilli beef kofta 74, **75**
chilli cheese slices 152, **153**
chilli cottage pie jackets 106, **107**, 204–5
coconut salmon bites 146, **147**
creamy sausage gnocchi 108, **109**, 205
crispy cauliflower tacos 58, **59**, 200
fajita crunchwrap 84, **85**, 202
hummus-crusted chicken 124, **125**
Mexican-style fish finger sandwich 68, **69**, 201
Moroccan-style tofu kebabs 92, **93**, 203
pea and ham croquettes 122, **123**, 206
peri-peri chicken nuggets 156, **157**, 207
pork and Parmesan burgers 80, **81**, 202
sweet chilli halloumi stuffed chicken **138**, 139, 206
Tex-Mex tacos 88, **89**, 203
salads
asparagus, broccoli and feta 170, **171**
Cajun-style steak 166, **167**
crispy chilli potato 164, **165**, 207
sprout and tahini **168**, 169
salmon
coconut salmon bites 146, **147**
harissa marmalade salmon **126**, 127
sriracha salmon with roasted pineapple salsa 96, **97**, 203–4
salsa
creamy 84, **85**, 202
roasted pineapple 96, **97**, 203–4
sandwiches
buffalo chicken 162, **163**, 207
Mexican-style fish finger 68, **69**, 201

sauces 16–17, 76, **77**
cheese 110–11, **111**, 205
ranch 56, **57**, 200
tomato **94**, 95, 203
sausage
cooking guide 31
creamy sausage gnocchi 108, **109**, 205
sage and rosemary traybake 132, **133**, 206
sesame seed
chicken and lemon noodles 64, **65**, 201
hummus-crusted chicken 124, **125**
sesame and ginger cod 136, **137**
sweet and sour crispy tofu 72, **73**, 201–2
slaw, cheesy 58, **59**, 200
soldiers and cheesy beans 36, **37**
soup, roasted tomato and garlic 174, **175**, 208
sourdough (wholemeal)
cherry cottage cheese toast 34, **35**
peanut butter and banana toast 50, **51**
spices 16
spinach
chicken and mango chutney traybake 104, **105**, 204
red pepper egg bites 52, **53**
sriracha salmon with roasted pineapple salsa 96, **97**, 203–4
steak
Cajun-style steak salad 166, **167**
steak bites and potatoes **128**, 129
Stilton
buffalo chicken sandwich 162, **163**, 207
dressing 166, **167**
stocks 16
strawberry, cloud pancakes 44–5, **45**, 200
strudel, chicken curry 100, **101**, 204
sumac chicken with roasted vegetables and herby couscous 130–1, **131**, 206
sun-dried tomato
pizza crumpets 154, **155**, 207
sun-dried tomato chicken bake 118, **119**, 205
vegetable crisps and dips 158, **160–1**
sweet potato
Indian-style sweet potato fries and raita 144, **145**, 207
smoky halloumi and sweet potato bake 114, **115**, 205
sweet and sour crispy tofu 72, **73**, 201–2
sweet treats 177–98, 208
sweetcorn 106, 166, 204–5
sweeteners 18

tacos
    crispy cauliflower 58, **59**, 200
    Tex-Mex 88, **89**, 203
tahini
    maple, date and tahini granola 38, **39**
    sprout and tahini salad **168**, 169
tart, beetroot and feta 116, **117**
tarte tatin, apricot 178, **179**
Tenderstem broccoli
    asparagus, broccoli and feta salad 170, **171**
    sausage, sage and rosemary traybake 132, **133**, 206
thickeners 17
tins 17, 21
toast
    cherry cottage cheese 34, **35**
    peanut butter and banana 50, **51**
toasties, eggy bread **40**, 41
tofu
    Moroccan-style tofu kebabs 92, **93**, 203
    sweet and sour crispy tofu 72, **73**, 201–2
tomato
    aubergine parmigiana **112**, 113
    Bolognese potato hash 120, **121**, 205
    Cajun-style steak salad 166, **167**
    chilli beef kofta 74, **75**
    chilli cottage pie jackets 106, **107**, 204–5
    creamy salsa 84, **85**, 202
    creamy sausage gnocchi 108, **109**, 205
    pesto chicken traybake 140, **141**, 206–7
    pesto egg bagels 42, **43**
    pork and Parmesan burgers 80, **81**, 202
    ranch burgers 56, **57**, 200
    roasted tomato and garlic soup 174, **175**, 208
    roasted vegetable pasta bake 134, **135**, 206
    smoky halloumi and sweet potato bake 114, **115**, 205
    spicy beef and chickpea flatbread 98, **99**, 204
    sun-dried tomato chicken bake 118, **119**, 205
    Tex-Mex tacos 88, **89**, 203
    see also passata; sun-dried tomato
tortilla chips, Mexican-style fish finger sandwich 68, **69**, 201
tortilla wraps
    fajita crunchwrap 84, **85**, 202
    Moroccan-style tofu kebabs 92, **93**, 203
    Tex-Mex tacos 88, **89**, 203
traybakes
    chicken and mango chutney 104, **105**, 204
    pesto chicken 140, **141**, 206–7
    sausage, sage and rosemary 132, **133**, 206
turkey, biryani-style 70, **71**, 201

vegetables
    cooking guide 30
    frozen 17
    roasted vegetable pasta bake 134, **135**, 206
    steamed vegetables 110–11, 114, 118, 205
    sumac chicken with roasted vegetables and herby couscous 130–1, **131**, 206
    vegetable crisps and dips 158, **160–1**

wraps 18
    crispy cauliflower tacos 58, **59**, 200
    see also tortilla wraps

yoghurt *see* Greek yoghurt

ACKNOWLEDGEMENTS

We owe many thank yous to many people who work so hard to bring this book together. Without these people, there would be no book. We deeply appreciate you all and can't thank you enough for the time and effort you put into making this book something we are immensely proud of.

We want to say a huge thank you firstly, to all of our followers on social media and all those who continue to make our recipes and let us know what you want next! We're so proud that Pinch of Nom has helped, and continues to help, so many people.

Thank you to our publisher Lizzy Gray. To Martha Burley, Bríd Enright, Rebecca Kellaway, Jodie Lancet-Grant, Dawn Burnett, Sarah Badhan, Amy Winchester and the rest of the team at Bluebird for helping us create this book and continuing to believe in Pinch of Nom throughout our journey. Major thanks also to our agent Clare Hulton for your unwavering support and guidance.

To Mike English for the amazing photos and to Kate Wesson, Kristine Jakobsson, Eden Owen-Jones and Daisy Shayler-Webb for making our food look so, so good. Thanks also to Georgia Rudd for all your assistance. Big thanks go out to Emma Wells and Nikki Dupin at Nic & Lou for making this book so beautiful!

We also want to thank our friends and family who have made this book possible. A very big thank you to Dr Hannah Cowan, Kirsty Rogers, Kenzie and Morgan. Your support has meant the world.

Special thanks go to Katie Mitchell and Rosie Sparrow for the endless hours you've put into this and for working so hard to get things right!

A huge thank you to our wonderful team of recipe developers who work tirelessly to help us bring these recipes to life; Lisa Allinson and Holly Levell.

Massive thanks also go to Sophie Fryer, Sophie Howarth, Hannah Cutting and Nick Nicolaou, for your writing and marketing support. To Cate Meadows and Jacob Lathbury for your creative and visual genius.

Additional thanks to Matthew Maney, Jessica Molyneux, Rubi Bourne and Vince Bourne for supporting us and the business – we are so proud to work alongside you all.

To our wonderful moderators and online support team; thank you for all your hard work keeping the peace and for all your support.

Furry thanks to Mildred, Wanda and Freda for the daily moments of joy.

And finally... huge thanks go to Paul and Cath Allinson for all your support and advice over the years. You are never forgotten. #YNWA

First published 2026 by Bluebird
an imprint of Pan Macmillan
The Smithson, 6 Briset Street, London EC1M 5NR
EU representative: Macmillan Publishers Ireland Ltd, 1st Floor,
The Liffey Trust Centre, 117–126 Sheriff Street Upper,
Dublin 1, D01 YC43

Associated companies throughout the world
www.panmacmillan.com

ISBN 978-1-0350-9015-0
Copyright © Kate and Kay Allinson, 2026

The right of Kate and Kay Allinson to be identified as the authors of this work has been asserted by them in accordance with the Copyright, Designs and Patents Act 1988.

All rights reserved. No part of this publication may be reproduced, stored in a retrieval system, or transmitted, in any form, or by any means (electronic, mechanical, photocopying, recording or otherwise) without the prior written permission of the publisher.

Pan Macmillan does not have any control over, or any responsibility for, any author or third-party websites referred to in or on this book.

9 8 7 6 5 4 3 2 1

A CIP catalogue record for this book is available from the British Library.

Photographer Mike English
Design, Illustration & Art Direction Emma Wells and Nikki Dupin, Studio Nic+Lou
Food Stylists Kristine Jakobsson and Kate Wesson
Prop Stylist Daisy Shayler-Webb

Printed and bound in Germany.

This book is sold subject to the condition that it shall not, by way of trade or otherwise, be lent, hired out, or otherwise circulated without the publisher's prior consent in any form of binding or cover other than that in which it is published and without a similar condition including this condition being imposed on the subsequent purchaser.

Visit www.panmacmillan.com to read more about all our books and to buy them. You will also find features, author interviews and news of any author events, and you can sign up for e-newsletters so that you're always first to hear about our new releases.

ABOUT PINCH OF NOM

Kate and Kay Allinson owned a restaurant together on the Wirral, where Kate was head chef. Together they created the Pinch of Nom blog with the aim of teaching people how to cook. They began sharing healthy, slimming recipes and today Pinch of Nom is the UK's most visited food blog with an active and engaged online community of over 4.5 million followers.

Also available from the no 1 bestselling authors:

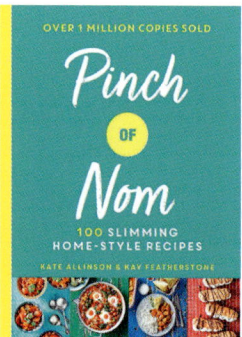  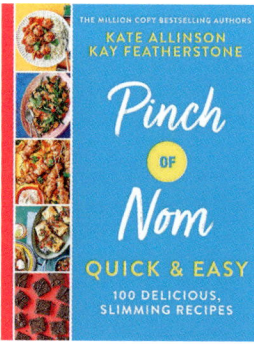 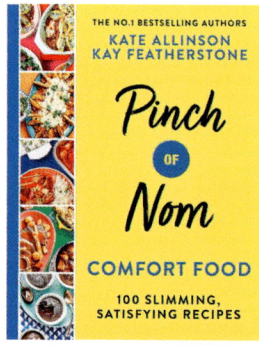

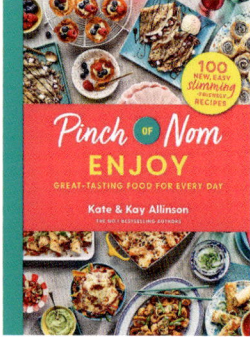  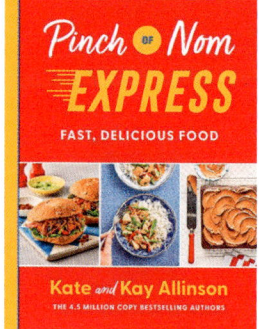 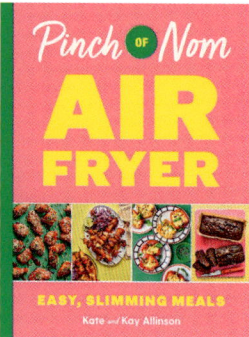

 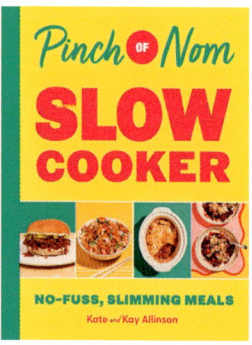